MW00964743

FROM THE LIBRARY OF

Clai Densley

The Tea
EXPERIENCE

The *Tea* EXPERIENCE

FAVORITE RECIPES FROM CELEBRATED TRAVEL DESTINATIONS

A publication of *TeaTime* magazine
Hoffman Media, LLC.
Birmingham, Alabama

Publisher: Phyllis Hoffman

Editor: Barbara Cockerham
Associate Editor: Stacey Norwood
Staff Writer: Amanda Manning
Contributing Writers: Andrea Fanning, Jennifer Kornegay, Teresa Hodges, Lucas Whittington

Test Kitchen Director: Rebecca Treadwell Touliatos
Food Editors: Aimee Bishop, Loren Wood

Creative Director: Mac Jamieson
Style Director: Yukie McLean
Photographers: Marcy Black, Kimberly Finkel Davis
Photo Stylist: Lindsay Keith Kessler

Production Director: Greg Baugh
Art Director: Karissa Brown
Copy Editor: Lucas Whittington
Color Technicians: Delisa McDaniel, Chris Waits

Copyright © 2007 by Hoffman Media, LLC.
Publishers of *TeaTime* magazine

All rights reserved. No part of this book may be reproduced or transmitted in any form or by any means, electronic or mechanical, including photocopying, or by any information storage and retrieval system, without permission in writing from Hoffman Media, LLC. Reviewers may quote brief passages.

First published in 2007 by Hoffman Media, LLC.
Birmingham, Alabama
With offices at:
1900 International Park Drive, Suite 50
Birmingham, Alabama 35243
www.hoffmanmedia.com

ISBN 978-0-9794090-0-4

CONTENTS

*Dedicated to tearoom owners who strive to
enhance each day with Afternoon Tea,
especially those whose work is included in these pages.*

INTRODUCTION

Traveling with tea in mind has become a favorite pastime of many. Why not plan our travel around the location of a cozy home-like tearoom, or choose a hotel because it offers exceptional Afternoon Tea?

One of the highlights for the staff of *TeaTime* magazine is being invited to visit a tearoom, try a new tea blend, and sample the scones, savories, and sweets. Since the magazine's inception, we have traveled the country in search of great tearooms, and we have found energizing teas in metropolitan settings and serene teas in quaint cottages.

Each tea experience should enhance your day, whether you seek solitude or congenial companionship. If tea at home is on the agenda, you'll need a well-stocked pantry, a fresh assortment of the best teas, and a collection of fabulous tea-food recipes. With proper preparation, taking tea at home will be as pleasurable as being served in your favorite tearoom.

The recipes within these pages are specialties from our favorite tea venues, and most are previously unpublished. You may find that these beautiful and delicious foods will become your favored specialties as you serve tea again and again.

THE TEA STORY

PHOTOGRAPHY BY ARDEN WARD

According to legend, the discovery of tea was an accident, an act of nature. A story handed down generation-to-generation gives credit for the finding to Chinese Emperor Shen Nung, a man concerned with matters of health and well-being.

He had observed that people who boiled water before drinking it suffered less from sicknesses, so he incorporated the extra step into his daily routine. The story continues that one day, around 2737 BC, the Emperor used wood from an evergreen plant, *Camellia sinensis*, for building a fire to heat water. When the wind blew a few leaves from the wood into the pot, a wonderful aroma enticed the Emperor to drink the resulting liquid, and tea was discovered.

Portuguese merchants, with established trade routes to the Far East, are credited with bringing tea to Lisbon. From Portugal, Dutch traders introduced the fragrant drink to other European countries, and England, where the very wealthy quickly adopted the beverage. It is said that Catherine of Braganza, wife of Charles II, brought tea as a part of her dowry from her homeland of Portugal and introduced the drink at court. What had begun in England as a luxury for the upper class eventually became the national drink in Great Britain by the mid-to-late 1600s. The Dutch established a direct trade with the Orient, forming the Dutch East India Company, and tea became more affordable to those outside the gentry class.

The serving of tea varied greatly from simple farmhouses to castles. Workers gathered in the cozy confines of a kitchen for thickly sliced, buttered bread, meat, cheese, and a thick slice of fruitcake, a meal deserved after a day spent in physical labor. In town, elegantly attired women and men met in finely appointed drawing rooms to partake of dainty sandwiches, perhaps of cucumber or watercress, and to sip tea served in delicate bone china cups filled from a silver teapot.

The practice of serving tea with food, in the afternoon between meals, is generally thought to have originated with Anna, the seventh Duchess of Bedford, who initiated the practice to ward off "sinking spells." At that time, meals consisted of a large breakfast, a light lunch, and a large dinner served around 8 or 9 p.m. The idea gained popularity and became known as Afternoon Tea.

Tea was exported to the Colonies by 1650, and in the New World, the custom of tea drinking became as popular as in England. Teatime became an opportunity to entertain, to display genteel manners, and associate with other members of society. Collecting tea wares was regarded as a symbol of wealth.

Making tea is simple; serving tea can be as complex as one wishes. To prepare for Afternoon Tea, gather together a tea pot, preferably heavy pottery for brewing the tea, and perhaps silver or china for serving; a tea cozy to help retain the heat of the pot; a tea strainer; cups and saucers (purists never use mugs); spoons; the requisite sugar, lemon and milk; and an array of tiny sandwiches, scones, and thinly sliced cake or bite-size sweets.

The tea story is timeless, a part of culture through the ages, and the story continues to evolve. This book, filled with recipes for delectable foods to accompany cup after cup of steaming hot tea, can be a useful part of your contribution to the tea story in your life.

APPLE CAKE TEA ROOM
Knoxville, Tennessee

Mary Henry views the Apple Cake Tea Room as an extension of her home, welcoming guests into a comfortable, relaxing environment.

"From the moment our guests enter the door, we want them to feel comfortable," Apple Cake Tea Room proprietor Mary Henry says with sincerity. She adds, "This is an extension of my home, and I want my guests to be able to come here, and relax and enjoy."

Bright smiles and cordial greetings immediately melt away worries of the road, as you begin to feel the warmth of hospitality that fills this little cabin from top to bottom. Handmade quilts and family heirlooms adorn the walls, items so familiar they bring to mind fond memories of visits to grandmother's house, and of stories told time and again—the kind that get better with each telling. Even the wooden floors seem glad to welcome you with their friendly creak as you're seated in a quaint dining room.

While you look over the menu, a server brings a tiny basket of delicious bran mini muffins and warm butter. Though you could eat only the melt-in-your-mouth muffins and be absolutely content, the menu is filled with items much too good to miss.

"Everything we make is fresh. There is always chicken cooking on the stove—our chicken salad is quite popular—and two bakers arrive at 8 a.m., preparing cakes, bread, and muffins," says Mary. "We've had basically the same menu since 1983, when we opened. We've added a few new things along the way, but one of the comments we hear most from our customers is that they're glad to find things haven't changed too much."

One of the most popular menu items, the Tea Room Medley, consists of chicken salad, glazed fruit, and a banana nut bread sandwich with cream cheese filling and chips. "This is one of our signatures," says Mary, explaining that the menu offers something for everyone.

"When I decided to do this to help put my children through college, I knew it had to be a very special place," says Mary. With an idea in mind of how she wanted the cabin to look, Mary struggled to find just the right name for her business. She says, "One day, everything just clicked. I was flipping through my mother's *Betty Crocker Cookbook*, and there it was, a recipe for apple cake"—just the inspiration she needed. Mary took the basic recipe and worked diligently to develop what is now the tearoom's namesake and most popular dessert.

Among the tearoom's special selections are spiced Friendship Tea—served hot or cold—and the Cornucopia; a rolled prizzelle filled with ice cream and sautéed bananas, drizzled with a choice of butterscotch or chocolate sauce. Another favorite is the warm Brownie Pie, piled high with ice cream and topped with chocolate sauce, perfect for sharing with a friend.

Sharing—it's what the Apple Cake Tea Room is all about. "We've had a lot of guests over the years," says Mary, "and I think the best compliment is that they keep coming back. The stories they tell me about this place—meeting their adopted son for the first time, rekindling a long-lost friendship; ladies who were once brought here by their mothers are now the ones bringing both their mothers and daughters . . . It brings me a lot of joy to bring joy to others."

ᏕᎧᏙ

Apple Cake Tea Room is located at 11312 Station West Drive, Knoxville, Tennessee. Tea is served daily, Monday through Saturday 11 a.m. to 2:30 p.m. For parties of five or more, reservations are requested. Call 865-966-7848.

~&~ RECIPES ~&~

APPLE CAKE'S BRAN MUFFINS • OLD FASHIONED SCONES
• "YOU THINK IT'S CRANBERRY BUT IT'S NOT" SALAD

Mary Henry's Apple Cake menu hasn't changed much since she opened the tearoom in 1983. The following recipes are some of her customers' favorites. You'll be surprised by the cranberry salad, a tasty treat that contains no cranberries.

To make an appetizing display of the Bran Muffins, stack the muffins pyramid-style on a vintage cake-pan. Place fresh cranberries around the base of the muffins to bring color to the display.

APPLE CAKE'S BRAN MUFFINS
Makes 32 muffins

1   cup boiling water
3   cups bran cereal
1   cup butter
1½   cups sugar
2   large eggs
2½   cups all-purpose flour
2½   teaspoons baking soda
1   teaspoon salt
2   cups buttermilk

1. Preheat oven to 400°. Line muffin pans with paper liners.
2. In medium bowl, pour boiling water over cereal; let stand.
3. In large bowl and using electric mixer at medium speed, beat together butter and sugar. Add eggs.
4. In medium bowl, sift together flour, baking soda, and salt.
5. Using electric mixer at medium speed, add dry ingredients to butter mixture, alternating with buttermilk. Add softened cereal and stir to combine thoroughly.
6. Fill muffin pans ²/₃ full with batter. Place in oven. Bake 15 minutes, or until wooden pick inserted near center comes out clean.

OLD FASHIONED SCONES
Makes 8 scones

2   cups all-purpose flour
1   tablespoon baking powder
2   tablespoons sugar
1/2 teaspoon salt
6   tablespoons butter
1/2 cup buttermilk
1   lightly beaten egg

1. Preheat oven to 425°.
2. In medium bowl, combine flour, baking powder, sugar, and salt. Using pastry blender, cut in butter until mixture is crumbly.
3. Form well in center of dough and add buttermilk. Stir until dough clings together and is sticky.
4. On lightly floured surface, flatten dough into 8-inch circle about 1½ inches thick. Working quickly, cut dough into wedges.
5. Place scones on ungreased baking sheet. Brush tops with beaten egg.
6. Bake 15 minutes, or until golden brown.

There's nothing more enticing than warm scones in a cloth-lined serving dish. These scones are ideal with just about any topping, from clotted cream to butter and beyond.

"YOU THINK IT'S CRANBERRY BUT IT'S NOT" SALAD
Makes 10 servings

2   (12-ounce) cans cola, divided
2   (3-ounce) boxes cherry gelatin mix
1   (20-ounce) can crushed pineapple
1   cup finely chopped pecans
Garnish: whipped cream

1. In medium saucepan over medium heat, bring 1 can cola to boil.
2. Add gelatin mix to cola, stirring to dissolve.
3. Add remaining cola.
4. Stir in pineapple and pecans, mixing well.
5. Pour mixture in 13x9x2-inch pan and refrigerate overnight. Serve, garnished with whipped cream, if desired.

Note: Sugar-free or diet cola may be substituted, if desired.

THE CAROLINA INN
Chapel Hill, North Carolina

PHOTOGRAPHY BY LEE THOMPSON

Beautiful mismatched china cups, saucers, and serving wares are used in counterpoint to each other for a stunning visual feast.

Taking tea at The Carolina Inn in Chapel Hill, North Carolina, is a bit like visiting your favorite aunt. Not the matronly variety, mind you, but rather the mysteriously glamorous *tante* who dotes on you—the kind who leaves a lasting impression. And although your favorite aunt may not be there to welcome you, the staff at the Inn will cater to your every whim. The Inn, listed as a historic hotel with The National Trust for Historic Preservation, is the epitome of elegance in a city graced with other century-old plantation-style homes.

Tea mistress Mary Susan Daniels and her serving staff attend to guests with care and courtesy, while Executive Chef Brian Stapleton and his kitchen associates preside over food preparation. The staff takes pride in presenting a memorable Afternoon Tea, from the freshly baked scones to what may well be the most luscious lemon curd this side of the Blue Ridge Mountains.

"Many think that because the "12 Days of Christmas" is so incredibly popular at the Inn and because our holiday tea is so enormously popular, that this is the only time of year we serve tea. Actually, tea is served Monday through Saturday, year-round, with seatings beginning at 3 p.m.," says Daniels.

Though the sweets and savories vary somewhat with the season, Chef Brian, who has mastered tea menus for more than two decades, insists that classic teatime cuisine is "classic" for a reason.

"Tea is tea, like chateaubriand is chateaubriand and beef Wellington is beef Wellington," he says.

The scones vary, according to Daniels, on the whim of the pastry chef. Favorite flavors include apricot ginger, currant, and sour cherry.

Choose the Classic Tea, or have the Royal Tea with a Champagne starter. A variety of teas from Taylors of Harrogate is offered to accompany the splendid foods.

Tea is served in the Inn's lobby, a comfortable home-like setting where a variety of tables and plush chairs invite you to linger. Antiques are used liberally, and the bright, feminine décor of the lobby proclaims Southern charm. Since part of the tea experience is the visual impression, the tea tables are adorned with beautiful mismatched vintage china cups and saucers, from nearby Replacements, Inc. in Greensboro.

"Sometimes I have two patterns used in counterpoint to each other. And at some tables, every guest will have a cup or teapot in a different china pattern. I also have some children's tea wares and teapots, especially for children who would have difficulty lifting a standard size teacup," notes Daniels.

Located on the campus of the University of North Carolina, The Carolina Inn is owned by the university, and all of its profits go to support the UNC libraries.

ഇൗരു

The Carolina Inn is located at 211 Pittsboro Street, Chapel Hill, North Carolina. Afternoon Tea is served daily, Monday through Saturday, 3 p.m. to 5 p.m. Reservations are required. Call 919-918-2777 for reservations or other information. www.carolinainn.com

RECIPES

HAM TEA SANDWICHES WITH HERBED CREAM CHEESE • DILLED CUCUMBER
TEA SANDWICHES • CHOCOLATE MOUSSE CUPS

The Carolina Inn is the epitome of elegance with its historical flourishes and luxurious accommodations. The service and foods continue this grand tradition. Not only are the following recipes pretty to look at, they are exquisite morsels you'll not soon forget.

Cutting the ham and bread at the same time allows for perfectly sized sandwiches. Fanned cornichons complete the look and taste.

HAM TEA SANDWICHES WITH HERBED CREAM CHEESE
Makes 12 sandwiches

1   (8-ounce) package cream cheese, softened
1   teaspoon salt
$1/2$ teaspoon ground black pepper
2   teaspoons finely chopped fresh parsley
2   teaspoons finely chopped fresh oregano
2   teaspoons finely chopped fresh thyme
3   slices white or whole wheat bread, crusts removed
3   slices ham, thinly sliced
1   tablespoon Dijon mustard
10-12 cornichons, sliced to fan

1. In medium bowl, combine cream cheese, salt, pepper, parsley, oregano, and thyme. Mix until well blended.
2. Toast bread on both sides; allow to cool slightly. Spread even amount of cream cheese mixture over each bread slice, and top with one slice ham. Using $2^1/2$-inch round cutter, cut sandwiches.
3. Place small dollop of Dijon mustard and sliced cornichon on top of each sandwich.

Instead of the traditional three-tiered tray, vary your serving wares to create an interesting look. Cut hydrangeas make a nice table garnish, and a cake stand is perfect for adding a little height to your sweet or savory selection.

DILLED CUCUMBER TEA SANDWICHES
Makes 9 sandwiches

1   (8-ounce) package cream cheese, softened
1   teaspoon salt
$^1/_2$ teaspoon ground black pepper
2   teaspoons finely chopped fresh parsley
2   teaspoons finely chopped fresh oregano
2   teaspoons finely chopped fresh thyme
3   slices white or whole wheat bread, crusts removed
1   medium cucumber, thinly sliced lengthwise
Garnish: sour cream, fresh dill sprigs

1. In medium bowl, combine cream cheese, salt, pepper, parsley, oregano, and thyme. Mix until well blended.
2. Spread even amount of cream cheese mixture over one side of each bread slice, and top with sliced cucumber, arranging like shingles. Slice into thirds. Garnish with small dollop of sour cream and sprigs of fresh dill, if desired.

Use a vegetable peeler to thinly slice cucumbers. Not only is it safer, but your slices will all be paper thin.

CHOCOLATE MOUSSE CUPS
Makes 24 pastries

24   (1$^1/_2$-inch) commercial pastry shells, thawed
1   cup semisweet chocolate chips
2   cups heavy cream, divided
Fresh raspberries

1. Prepare pastry shells according to package instructions.
2. In medium bowl, place chocolate chips.
3. In small saucepan, bring 1 cup cream to boil; pour over chocolate chips. Let stand 5 minutes to melt chocolate. Stir until smooth and cool to room temperature.
4. In medium bowl and using electric mixer at high speed, beat remaining cream until stiff peaks form. Fold into chocolate mixture.
5. Pipe or spoon mousse into pastry shells. Place fresh raspberry in center of each.

1891 CEDAR CREST VICTORIAN INN
Asheville, North Carolina

Bruce and Rita Wightman welcome you to the Cedar Crest Inn, one of Fodor's "Best Inns of the South."

Just four miles from the winding Blue Ridge Parkway sits Cedar Crest Victorian Inn, a Crayola-colored Queen Anne structure built for Charleston, South Carolina native William Breese. The magnificent example of Victorian architecture, surrounded by four acres of manicured grounds, is listed on the National Register of Historic Places. Located just three blocks from the legendary Biltmore Estate, the charming inn remains outfitted with authentic period antiques and stunning signature interior woodwork, shaped by many of the same artisans and craftsmen employed to build George W. Vanderbilt's palatial home.

Owned by Bruce and Rita Wightman, the bed and breakfast is an exquisite study in both ambience and pampering, and has the awards to prove it, including a starring spot in Fodor's "Best Inns of the South" and kudos from the Association of Historic Inns. One stay with the Wightmans and it's easy to see why.

The day begins with a full, gourmet breakfast that might include peaches and cream French toast or one of the house specialties, eggs goldenrod.

The day continues with Afternoon Tea, served to inn guests on the veranda in spring and summer, and in the parlor or dining room in fall and winter. Upon request, guests can enjoy tea in the privacy of their own room. "The tea food varies from season to season, and is dependent on the local produce available. For example, in fall we might have apple scones," says Rita.

The food, including an end-of-the-day bedside treat that varies from chocolate-dipped strawberries to triple-chocolate cookies, is prepared by Bruce, the quiet master of the kitchen and author of the inn's cookbook, and is served with a smile by either Rita or a member of her equally friendly staff. And should a guest need anything, including a button secretly sewn back on, a jacket pressed while you're not looking, or the use of the Internet after hours, the Wightmans will more than accommodate—they will thank you for the pleasure of serving you in a business they have come to love in the past 20 years.

ΣΟΩ

1891 Cedar Crest Victorian Inn is located at 674 Biltmore Avenue, Asheville, North Carolina. Call 800-252-0310 or 828-252-1389 for reservations.

RECIPES

WILLOW BROOK CHICKEN SALAD • PINEAPPLE PECAN QUICK BREAD
• LEMON BASIL BUTTER COOKIES

The food served with tea at the Cedar Crest Inn is as delightful as the establishment. Fine taste abounds, be it in the décor, the manicured grounds, or the food itself.

Willow Brook Chicken Salad only has five ingredients but they combine to create a complex taste that is great served alone, with crackers, or as a sandwich.

WILLOW BROOK CHICKEN SALAD
Makes 6 servings

4   medium skinless and boneless chicken breasts
1   cup mayonnaise
1   small onion, finely chopped
1½ teaspoons Mrs. Dash Seasoning Blend
1½ cups seedless red grape halves

1. In large saucepan, place chicken breasts in water to cover. Bring to boil, reduce temperature, and cook over low heat until tender. Remove from heat, drain, and cool.
2. Cut chicken into ½-inch pieces. Add mayonnaise, onion, and seasoning blend; mix gently.
3. Fold in grapes; refrigerate several hours to blend flavors.

PINEAPPLE PECAN QUICK BREAD
Makes 1 loaf

¾   cup firmly packed brown sugar
¼   cup shortening
1   large egg
2   cups all-purpose flour
1   teaspoon baking soda
½   teaspoon salt
⅓   cup orange juice
1   (8.25-ounce) can crushed pineapple in syrup
½   cup chopped pecans

1. Preheat oven to 350°. Grease bottom only of 9x5x3-inch loaf pan.

2. In large bowl and using electric mixer at medium speed, beat brown sugar and shortening until light and creamy; beat in egg. Stir in flour, baking soda, salt and orange juice. Stir in pineapple with syrup and pecans. Pour batter into prepared pan.

3. Bake 50-55 minutes, or until wooden pick inserted near center comes out clean.

4. Cool slightly in pan. Loosen sides of loaf from pan; remove to wire rack and allow to cool completely before slicing.

Note: To store, wrap and refrigerate up to 1 week.

LEMON BASIL BUTTER COOKIES
Makes about 6½ dozen cookies

1	cup fresh basil leaves
1¾	cups sugar, divided
2	cups butter, softened
¼	cup fresh lemon juice
1	large egg
6	cups all-purpose flour

1. Preheat oven to 350°. Lightly grease baking sheet.

2. In work bowl of food processor, combine basil and ¼ cup sugar. Pulse until blended.

3. In large bowl and using electric mixer at medium speed, beat butter until creamy. Gradually add 1½ cups sugar, and beat well. Add lemon juice and egg, beating until blended. Add flour, 1 cup at a time, until incorporated; beat until dough is stiff.

4. Shape mixture into 1-inch balls and place 2 inches apart on prepared baking sheet. Flatten slightly with bottom of drinking glass dipped in sugar.

5. Bake 12 minutes, or until lightly browned. Cool on wire rack.

The chef at 1891 Cedar Crest Victorian Inn puts a new spin on breakfast bread. Pineapples paired with pecans make a quick bread that is great for Afternoon Tea as well as breakfast.

CHARLESTON PLACE
Charleston, South Carolina

Impeccable service is just one of the reasons to take tea at Charleston Place hotel. The finest teas and delectable savories and scones are beyond compare.

Perhaps the most renowned tea experience in Charleston—and rightfully so—is the impeccable service that awaits tea lovers at Charleston Place hotel.

The hotel's Thoroughbred Club delights in the unhurried pace of its English-style Afternoon Tea, as well as its tradition of quality. With seatings available by reservation only, guests may opt for the Charleston Classic Tea or the South of Broad Tea, which includes a Champagne starter—both are accompanied by warming pots of premium tea from the hotel's chosen providers, Harney & Sons and Taylors of Harrogate.

"We pride ourselves on serving only the world's best teas, with over 25 selections to choose from. Our delectable open-face tea sandwiches are second to none. Our in-house pastry chef bakes fresh fruit-filled scones daily. Dainty pastries and petit fours served on the finest Austrian-made china round out the experience," says food and beverage manager Stewart Moore.

The choice of scones, like the rest of the menu, is largely dependent on the season. In summer, that might be "cherries and berries," while in colder months, chocolate chip, or raisin and cinnamon. Another traditional tea bread offering served at Charleston Place, and one not commonly found on many American tea menus, is fresh, golden crumpets. These, like the scones, may be enjoyed with guests' choice of honey, preserves, kitchen-fresh lemon curd, and dollops of whipped cream.

Savories and sweets are as fresh as the lemon curd, and are prepared daily. Ocean-fresh shrimp and lobster are typically among the savories served, along with finger sandwiches such as roast beef with olive tapenade and horseradish cream. The array of sweets ranges from opera torte to fresh fruit tarts and cobblers, and like the savories, is intended by the culinary team to please the eye as well as the palate.

In addition to its daily Afternoon Tea offerings, the Thoroughbred Club also hosts several specialty tea services throughout the year, including a Yuletide Tea at Christmas and the popular Teddy Bear Tea for children. Festive treats such as stollen and the seasonal White Christmas Blend—white tea blended with almonds, vanilla, cardamom, and white chamomile flowers—help make the Yuletide Tea a popular annual event at the Thoroughbred Club, just as the Teddy Bear Tea introduces a new generation of young ladies and gentlemen each year to the pleasures of Afternoon Tea.

Along with a visit from St. Nick, youngsters also enjoy such entertainment as magic shows and storytelling while quenching their thirst with their choice of warm apple juice, hot chocolate, or chocolate milk accompanied by bear-shaped peanut butter and jelly sandwiches, hot scones, and more.

Such unwavering attention to detail and respect for tradition, says Stewart, is the standard at the Thoroughbred Club. "The unhurried Southern hospitality combined with the incredible food makes teatime at Charleston Place hotel an experience not to be missed."

ℰᘏᘐ

Charleston Place is located at 205 Meeting Street, Charleston, South Carolina. Secured reservations are recommended for tea, served 1 p.m. to 4 p.m., Monday through Saturday. Call 843-722-4900, extension 7689. www.charlestonplace.com.

RECIPES

PESTO CREAM CHEESE TEA SANDWICHES • ALMOND SCONES
• PISTACHIO MINI MUFFINS

The open-face Pesto Cream Cheese Tea Sandwiches are a specialty of Charleston Place. Pistachio Mini Muffins and Almond Scones bring a nutty flavor to the tea table.

Other garnishes to consider include roasted red pepper strips, a bit of pancetta, or shaved turkey.

PESTO CREAM CHEESE TEA SANDWICHES
Makes 24 sandwiches

2   (8-ounce) packages cream cheese, softened
1¼ cup spinach or watercress blanched, chopped, and squeezed dry
½   cup diced red bell pepper
½   cup diced yellow bell pepper
3   cloves garlic, minced
½   cup sour cream
2   tablespoons prepared pesto
½   teaspoon salt
¼   teaspoon ground black pepper
6   slices wheat bread, crusts removed
Garnish: grape tomatoes, cucumbers, micro-sprouts

1. In large mixing bowl, combine cream cheese, spinach or watercress, bell peppers, garlic, sour cream, and pesto. Add salt and pepper.
2. Cover mixture and refrigerate for at least 30 minutes.
3. Cut bread slices into quarters. Spread Pesto Cream Cheese on each quarter.
4. Garnish with thinly sliced grape tomato, cucumber and micro-sprouts, if desired.

Note: Remaining Pesto Cream Cheese can be stored in airtight container in refrigerator for at least a week.

ALMOND SCONES
Makes 56 mini scones

2   cups cake flour
1½ cups bread flour
¼   cup sugar
⅛   teaspoon salt
3¼ teaspoons baking powder
1¼ cups sliced almonds
¾   cup butter, cubed
1¼ cups heavy cream
2   large eggs

1. Preheat oven to 350°.
2. In large mixing bowl, combine cake flour, bread flour, sugar, salt, baking powder, and almonds.
3. Using pastry blender, cut in butter. Add cream and eggs. Mix dough just until combined.
4. Roll dough into thumb-size balls and place on baking sheets.
5. Bake 14-16 minutes, or until golden brown.

PISTACHIO MINI MUFFINS
Makes 20 mini muffins

2   cups flour
1   teaspoon baking soda
6   tablespoons butter
1¼ cups sugar
1   teaspoon salt
2   large eggs
1   cup sour cream
⅓   cup pistachio paste
1¼ cups ground pistachios
Garnish: confectioners' sugar

1. Preheat oven to 350°. Grease mini muffin pans.
2. In medium bowl, sift together flour and baking soda. In separate medium bowl and using electric mixer at medium speed, beat together butter, sugar, and salt. Add eggs and beat until well blended. Add flour mixture, beating just until moistened.
3. Beat in sour cream, scraping down sides often.
4. Add pistachio paste and ground pistachios, beating to mix well.
5. Spoon batter into prepared pans, filling each well about ⅔ full.
6. Bake 20 minutes, or until wooden pick inserted near center comes out clean. Cool 10 minutes; remove to wire racks and cool completely. Garnish with confectioners' sugar, if desired.

These bite-sized treats are perfect for Afternoon Tea. If there are any leftovers, they make perfect grab-and-go breakfast snacks.

THE ENGLISH ROSE TEA ROOM
Chattanooga, Tennessee

The friendly, mostly British staff welcomes you into the English Rose Tea Room. Here you'll find a relaxing atmosphere with an authentic English influence.

From the moment you enter The English Rose Tea Room, cares melt away as the word "welcome" becomes more than a greeting. It's the feeling that completely surrounds you and continually warms your heart as you prepare for an afternoon of sheer delight.

Located in Chattanooga, Tennessee's pedestrian-friendly downtown, this charming tearoom is housed inside a historic brick building that was once the Grand Hotel. But the hustle and bustle of guests moving about the busy lobby has long since faded away, replaced by the peaceful hum of friendly conversation and the soft clinking of tea cups and saucers.

"The majority of our staff is British," says owner Angela Becksvoort, who is a native of the British colony Zimbabwe—now Rhodesia—and long-time resident of Surrey. "But even more than that, we are all really good friends." And it shows. The engaging environment paired with the unmistakable British influence is truly what makes this tearoom such a delight. It is also exactly the kind of place Angela wanted it to be.

"I wanted this to be a place where people could come to enjoy each other's company," she says. Though her background was in nursing, a pursuit that brought her to the United States, Angela found that opening a tearoom was a way to combine her love for her homeland with her desire to care for others. She says, "I'd never done anything like this before, but I felt there was a place for it here in the South."

"I decided it was important that we had Royal Doulton china. After that, I focused on gentle colors and some of the Victorian influence, but I didn't stick to a specific time period," says Angela, explaining that she also wanted to highlight the building's grand heritage and architecture. "I didn't want anything that would be stuffy or stand-offish. It was really more about having something nice, with good china, good cutlery, and good linens. And most importantly, everything needed to be absolutely English."

Crumpets, cottage pies, Cornish pasties—the menu ranges from traditional tea to pub-style lunches. Both the Afternoon Tea and the Victorian Tea are served throughout the day. Each includes the choice of assorted finger sandwiches, English biscuits, and a scone served with Devon cream, strawberry jam, and lemon curd, along with a pot of tea. The Victorian Tea also offers English cheeses with crackers as well as a dessert. And there are many delicious delights to choose from, such as Sherry Trifle, Sticky Toffee Pudding, and, a tearoom favorite, Eton Chaos.

Adding a taste of Britain to events and celebrations is another English Rose specialty. Angela says, "We host children's tea parties, etiquette classes, and receptions. We've even had weddings here—small, intimate weddings where they get married on the stairs—just lovely. We celebrate British traditions and holidays, and at Christmastime we host a series of special teas."

ℰ⃝ℛ

The English Rose Tea Room is located at 1401 Market Street, Chattanooga, Tennessee. Tearoom service is available Monday through Saturday, 10 a.m. to 5:30 p.m., and the gift shop remains open until 6 p.m. Reservations are required for parties of 6 or more. Call 423-265-5900.

RECIPES

CHEESE STRAWS • CREAM SCONES • ETON CHAOS

Alongside traditional English tea fare, The English Rose Tea Room also offers a Southern favorite—Cheese Straws. This recipe substitutes caraway seeds for cayenne pepper, giving them a nutty, sophisticated taste.

Everything from the British accents of the staff, to the Royal Doulton china will whisk you from Chattanooga to the British Isles, even if it's only for a respite.

CHEESE STRAWS
Makes 24 cheese straws

1½ (15-ounce) refrigerated pie crusts
1   large egg, lightly beaten
¼   cup finely grated Cheddar cheese
¼   cup finely grated Swiss cheese
1   tablespoon caraway seeds

1. Preheat oven to 400°. Lightly grease baking sheet.
2. On lightly floured surface, unroll pie crusts. Brush with egg and sprinkle with Cheddar cheese, Swiss cheese, and caraway seeds.
3. Cut crusts into 6x½-inch-wide strips. Twist strips into corkscrew shapes. Place 1 inch apart on prepared baking sheet.
4. Bake 7-10 minutes or until golden brown. Serve hot or cold.

Note: Cheese straws may be stored for several days in an airtight container. Reheat in 300° oven.

CREAM SCONES
Makes 12 scones

2   cups all-purpose flour
2   teaspoons baking powder
2   teaspoons sugar
½   teaspoon salt
¼   cup butter, cubed
3   large eggs, lightly beaten and divided
⅓   cup half-and-half
2   tablespoons sugar

1. Preheat oven to 400°. Lightly grease baking sheet.
2. In medium bowl, sift together flour, baking powder, sugar, and salt. Using pastry mixer, cut in butter until mixture is crumbly.
3. In small bowl, combine 2 eggs and half-and-half. Add to flour mixture, stirring just until dry ingredients are moistened.
4. On lightly floured surface, roll dough to ¾-inch thickness. Using 2½-inch cutter, cut scones. Place scones on prepared baking sheet. Brush tops of scones with remaining egg. Sprinkle with sugar.
5. Bake 12-15 minutes, or until golden brown.

ETON CHAOS
Makes 6-8 servings

2   egg whites
¼   teaspoon cream of tartar
½   cup sugar
2   cups heavy cream
⅓   cup confectioners' sugar
2   cups chopped strawberries
Garnish: fresh mint sprigs, strawberries

1. Preheat oven to 225°. Line baking sheet with parchment paper.
2. In medium bowl and using electric mixer at high speed, beat egg whites to stiff peaks. Add cream of tartar; gradually beat in sugar. Drop meringues in egg-size mounds onto prepared baking sheet. Bake 2½ hours.
3. In medium bowl and using electric mixer at medium speed, beat cream until soft peaks form. Add confectioners' sugar; beat until stiff peaks form. Crumble meringues into chips.
4. Combine cream, strawberries, and meringue chips. Garnish with fresh mint and strawberries, if desired.

Note: Meringues can be made up to a week in advance. Store in airtight container to maintain crispness.

Strawberries, meringue, and whipped cream combine to make Eton Chaos, one of The English Rose's signature desserts.

THE FAIRMONT OLYMPIC HOTEL
Seattle, Washington

Come out of the rain and enjoy the tea experience at the Georgian, located at the Fairmont Olympic Hotel in downtown Seattle.

Though perhaps best known for its abundance of yearly rainfall, Seattle also showers its visitors with a multitude of unique opportunities, including the chance to delve into the depths of a most charming tea experience.

Towering evergreens, soaring mountain peaks, lush foliage—every mile along the road to Seattle, Washington, unfurls and unfolds into a multitude of scenic marvels. You see the city skyline from afar, the unmistakable Space Needle reaching towards the gently drifting clouds above. Along the waterfront, sailboats glide on the gales, and in the distance, ferryboats carry on with their daily jaunts, leaving rhythmically rolling wakes in their paths. It is in the midst of this maritime masterpiece that you plan to spend your day.

The highlight of your time here is undoubtedly taking tea at The Georgian, located in the heart of downtown in the prestigious Fairmont Olympic Hotel. Only a few blocks away from the famed Pike Place Market—one of the nation's oldest continuously running farmers' markets—noted for its fresh fish, produce, and flowers, along with a variety of antiques, collectibles, and arts and crafts—the Fairmont is a destination in and of itself.

From the moment you step onto hotel premises, you are treated like royalty. Exquisite Italian Renaissance architecture paired with elegantly appointed decorative accents

The Fairmont Olympic has evolved from the grandest inn west of Chicago in 1924 to Washington's only AAA Five Diamond hotel (earning its 22nd consecutive Five Diamond designation in 2006).

result in a stately yet inviting atmosphere, and you can't help but notice the abundance of floral arrangements, each one absolutely breathtaking. A pleasant chat with a hotel employee reveals that these fragrant beauties are assembled on the premises daily. Continuing through the distinguished lobby, you make your way to The Georgian, one of the hotel's three restaurants.

Since opening in 1924, the Fairmont Olympic has been a landmark for this region's prominent civic and social events, and today you have the chance to partake in that tradition. You give the name for your reservation, and a cheerful hostess guides you through the opulent dining room to a lovely table. Amiable conversations faintly fill the grand room with a sound much like the delicate and melodic jingling of bells. Adding to the ambience, impressive chandeliers reflect The Fairmont's attention to luxury, and the rich draperies, crisp linens and Royal Doulton china only add to the finery. But the best is yet to come—the menu.

First comes the selection of loose leaf teas—the choices range from traditional Earl Grey to The Georgian's signature Kea Lani Orange Pineapple. Also specific to the hotel is the Empress Blend 1908, brewed to perfection with bright floral notes and hints of oak. For those seeking something more region-specific, there's a peppermint tisane with a cool and lively taste from the Cascade Mountains.

A tiered tray of incredibly enticing sandwiches, scones, and sweets soon arrives at your table, and the next—and perhaps most perplexing—decision is simply where to begin. Incorporating Seattle's mainstay, seafood, into the menu, The Georgian's chef strives to create unique flavors that evoke the essence of the city. Smoked Salmon with Avocado Butter, Shaved Fennel and Ikura Caviar or Dungeness Crab and Grapefruit Salad on Pain de Campagne—such tempting offerings lend to the tearoom's stellar reputation.

Seasonal scones are served with delicious Devonshire cream and preserves. A series of sweets rounds out the sampling, each one a miniature work of art. Spun sugar, chocolate curls and fresh berries garnish the various delectables that include Granny Smith Apple Delight, Chocolate Brandy Crisp, Sugared Coconut Macaroon, and the never-disappointing Classic Fresh Fruit Tart.

You leave the Fairmont Olympic and step back into the streets of Seattle, rested, relaxed, renewed and ready to see what else this seafaring city has to offer.

ΣΟΩ

The Fairmont Olympic Hotel is located at 411 University Street, Seattle, Washington. Afternoon Tea at The Georgian is served daily from 11:30 a.m. to 2:30 p.m. Reservations are recommended and can be made by calling the Fairmont Olympic Hotel at 206-621-1700, extension 3169. www.fairmont.com/seattle

RECIPES

LOBSTER CHOP-CHOP ON GRILLED CORNBREAD • POLENTA TEA BREAD
• CHOCOLATE TRUFFLE CAKES

Corn makes a surprise appearance on the menu at the Fairmont. A luscious lobster mixture tops grilled cornbread rounds, and the tea bread, made using cornmeal, resembles polenta. Serve the hotel's signature Chocolate Truffle Cakes as the tea finale.

Not a fan of lobster? Not a problem. Substitute either fresh crab or boiled shrimp.

LOBSTER CHOP-CHOP ON GRILLED CORNBREAD
Makes 12 sandwiches

$1^1/_2$ pounds lobster meat, finely diced
$^1/_2$ cup mayonnaise
2 tablespoons finely diced red onion
2 tablespoons finely diced celery
2 tablespoons finely diced red bell pepper
2 tablespoons finely diced yellow bell pepper
1 tablespoon chopped chives
1 tablespoon lemon juice
Salt and ground black pepper to taste
Cornbread (recipe follows)
Garnish: fine chiffonade of fresh basil

1. In medium bowl, combine lobster meat, mayonnaise, onion, celery, peppers, chives, and lemon juice. Season to taste with salt and pepper.
2. Using 2-inch round cutter, cut cornbread and trim to about $^1/_2$ inch thick. Grill or toast cornbread rounds; allow to cool.
3. Using same round cutter, mold lobster mixture on top of cornbread rounds about ¾ inch high. Garnish with chiffonade of fresh basil, if desired.

CORNBREAD

1	cup stone-ground cornmeal
1	cup all-purpose flour
2	teaspoons baking powder
1/4	teaspoon salt
3	tablespoons sugar
1	tablespoon baking soda
1	large egg
1 1/2	cups buttermilk

1. Preheat oven to 350°. Grease 13x9x2-inch baking pan.

2. In medium bowl, sift together cornmeal, flour, baking powder, salt, sugar, and baking soda. In small bowl, combine egg and buttermilk.

3. Add egg mixture to cornmeal mixture and mix thoroughly, adding more buttermilk if necessary to make smooth batter (this will depend on cornmeal texture).

4. Spread batter evenly into prepared pan. Bake 15-20 minutes, or until wooden pick inserted near `center comes out clean and cornbread is firm and golden brown.

POLENTA TEA BREAD
Makes 2 loaves

2 1/4	cups butter, softened
2 1/2	cups sugar
6	large eggs
1	teaspoon vanilla extract
1	cup sour cream
2	cups bread flour
1/4	teaspoon salt
1	cup plain yellow cornmeal
1/4	teaspoon baking soda

The Polenta Tea Bread recipe makes two loaves—one for serving now, and one for later. Wrap one loaf in plastic wrap and freeze for up to three months. Thaw overnight before serving.

1. Preheat oven to 375°. Spray two 9x5x3-inch loaf pans with non-stick cooking spray.

2. In large bowl and using electric mixer at medium speed, combine butter and sugar, mixing thoroughly. Add eggs, vanilla extract, and sour cream; beat 1 minute.

3. In medium bowl, sift together flour, salt, cornmeal, and baking soda. Add flour mixture to butter mixture; mixing until well combined. ·

4. Divide batter evenly between prepared loaf pans.

5. Bake 45-50 minutes, or until golden brown and springy in the middle. Loosely cover pans with aluminum foil during last 15 minutes of baking to prevent over-browning. Cool before slicing.

CHOCOLATE TRUFFLE CAKES
Makes about 12 cakes

1   cup bittersweet chocolate
³/₄ cup unsalted butter
2   large eggs
7   egg yolks
³/₄ cup sugar
3   tablespoons all-purpose flour, sifted
Garnish: confectioners' sugar

1. Preheat oven to 375°. Coat mini popover pan with nonstick cooking spray with flour.

2. In top of double boiler, melt chocolate with butter.

3. In medium bowl and using electric mixer at medium speed, beat eggs, yolks, and sugar approximately 1½ minutes, being careful not to over-beat. Add egg mixture to chocolate mixture, stirring to combine. Fold in flour.

4. Fill wells of prepared pan ²/₃ full with mixture. Let stand in pan 10 minutes.

5. Bake 15-20 minutes, or until wooden pick inserted near center comes out clean. Cool, remove from pans.

6. Garnish with confectioners' sugar, if desired.

Dusted with confectioners' sugar and served with fresh raspberries and chocolate sauce, these fudgy cakes are a rich, decadent dessert.

FOUR SEASONS HOTEL
Philadelphia, Pennsylvania

Delectable sweets, prepared in individual serving sizes, are a hallmark of the tea foods served at the Swann Lounge in Four Seasons Hotel in one of the nation's oldest cities.

In the city called both "the birthplace of America" and "the city of brotherly love," tea is as near as the timeless and ever-tasteful Four Seasons Hotel, located at One Logan Square. Built overlooking one of the five original squares incorporated into William Penn's design for Philadelphia, the hotel provides stellar service in lodging, dining, and, for the tea aficionado, Afternoon Tea. In the hotel's elegant Swann Lounge, overlooking Alexander Stirling Calder's stunning Swann Memorial Fountain—representing the three rivers of Philadelphia as ancient river gods—awaits a not-to-be-missed tea experience.

Afternoon Tea, served using the hotel's custom designed Fortessa & Bernardaud Limoges china, promises to be the highlight of your day. Though the menu follows the standard order of service—savories, scones, and sweets—the food is hardly typical.

Tea is impeccably served by attendants whose goal is to give each guest a special experience. With an array of delectable finger sandwiches, scones served with clotted cream, preserves, and lemon curd, and beautiful taste-tempting sweets to crown the experience, the goal is easily attained. For special occasions, or to celebrate an ordinary day, choose the Royal Tea for the addition of sparkling wine, a raspberry cocktail, or sweet sherry to accompany the tea delicacies. The scones, sweets, and savories can also be ordered á la carte to complement your pot of freshly brewed Harney & Sons tea. Select your favorite blend, or

choose one of the Swann Lounge's most popular teas. Earl Grey, English Breakfast, and decaf Ceylon are favored black teas, with Jasmine as the most frequently chosen green tea. Herbals, such as chamomile and peppermint, are also available.

Sandwiches and sweets are prepared daily by the Four Seasons' chefs, with a nod to both seasonal ingredients and the guests' preferences. Favorite tea sandwiches include the Philadelphia Cream Cheese and Watercress on House-Baked White Bread, Rice-Wine flavored Cucumber and Butter on Brioche, and House-Smoked Salmon, Cream Cheese, and Dill on Whole Wheat Bread.

The three-tiered tray includes elegant sweets such as luscious strawberries dipped in chocolate, and fondant cakes. The scone selection is updated monthly, with favorites that include Scottish Scones, Cranberry Orange Scones, and Oatmeal Walnut Scones.

It is easy to settle into the comfortable lounge area and make memories while you enjoy the ceremony of tea, lulled by live music from the grand piano, or by the harpist who plays Tuesday through Saturday.

ନ୍ଦୁର

Four Seasons Hotel is located at One Logan Square, Philadelphia, Pennsylvania. Afternoon Tea is served from 3:00 p.m. to 4:30 p.m. Monday through Saturday. Reservations are recommended. Call 215-963-1500 for reservations. www.fourseasons.com/philadelphia

RECIPES

SMOKED SALMON SANDWICHES • GINGER LEMON SCONES
• ALMOND FINANCIERS

When the Swann Lounge chef plans the foods to be prepared each day, he is mindful of the availability of seasonal ingredients and the preferences of the hotel's guests. Many of the favored savories and sweets are timeless, and served year-round.

Watercress blended with cream cheese adds a peppery bite to the ever-popular smoked salmon used for petite sandwiches.

SMOKED SALMON SANDWICHES
Makes 12 sandwiches

$3/4$ cup cream cheese, softened to room temperature
1   cup watercress
6   slices wheat bread, crusts removed
1   (3-ounce) package smoked salmon, cut into 12 slices

1. In small bowl and using electric mixer at medium speed, beat cream cheese until creamy; add watercress and mix thoroughly.
2. Spread cream cheese mixture on 3 slices bread. Top with smoked salmon.
3. Cover with remaining bread and cut each sandwich into quarters.

GINGER LEMON SCONES
Makes 18 Scones

$2^1/2$ cups all purpose flour
5   tablespoons sugar
1   teaspoon salt
4   teaspoons baking powder
3   tablespoons fresh lemon zest
10 tablespoons butter

½	cup candied ginger, cut into small pieces
¼	cup milk
¼	cup buttermilk
1	egg
1	tablespoon heavy cream
Sugar	

1. Preheat oven to 400°. Line baking sheet with parchment paper.
2. In large bowl, combine flour, sugar, salt, baking powder, and lemon zest. Using pastry blender, cut in butter until mixture is crumbly. Stir in candied ginger.
3. In small bowl, whisk together milk, buttermilk, and egg. Make a well in center of flour mixture and pour milk mixture into center. Mix until just combined.
4. On floured surface, knead dough 3-4 times, to form a ball. Roll dough to ½-inch thickness. Using 2-inch round cutter, cut scones. Place scones 1 inch apart on prepared baking sheet. Brush scones with cream and sprinkle with sugar. Bake 15 minutes or until golden brown.

ALMOND FINANCIERS
Makes 24 pastries

¾	cup butter
1¾	cups confectioners' sugar
½	cup plus 1 tablespoon all purpose flour
½	cup finely ground almonds
5	egg whites
Confectioners' sugar	

1. Preheat oven to 325°. Grease and flour mini muffin pans.
2. In small saucepan over medium heat, brown butter.
3. In work bowl of electric mixer fitted with paddle attachment, combine confectioners' sugar, flour, and almonds; mix at low speed.
4. In small bowl, gently whisk egg whites. Add egg whites to sugar mixture; mix at low speed to combine. Add browned butter to mixture, mixing at low speed until combined. Increase mixer speed to medium for 1 minute.
5. Pour batter into prepared pans, filling each well half-full. Bake 15 minutes, or until set. Remove from oven and cool.
6. Remove from muffin pans and dust with confectioners' sugar.

Teatime would not be complete without the addition of a favorite scone. At Four Seasons' Swann Lounge, a popular scone combines lemon and ginger for a palate-pleasing taste.

GRACIE'S ENGLISH TEAROOM
Montgomery, Alabama

A full selection of fine teas and tea foods await guests at Gracie's English Rose Tea Room. Friendly and hospitable, Gracie's offers more than a cup of tea. According to owner Judy Gray, they offer a "cup of comfort."

Step inside Gracie's English Tearoom and the cares of the world seem to quickly drift away. The soft scents of tea and fresh-baked delights perfume the air, while light chatter punctuated by laughter fills the intimate rooms.

Set in a quaint old house in Montgomery's Mulberry District, Gracie's has a gentle grace and cheery comfort that evoke simpler times, but the establishment is not without a sense of elegance and style. The phrase "Practice and Pursue Hospitality" adorns the space above the front windows, and Gracie's certainly follows that imperative as the friendly staff greets guests. Almost every nook and cranny is filled with tea sets, inspirational books, and gifts as well as bright tins of fine, loose teas for sale. For those who want to add a whimsical flair to Afternoon Tea, there is even a rack holding colorful hats, each ready to add a special touch to tea.

Judy Gray opened Gracie's in December 2001 after retiring from a 29-year teaching career. She dreamed of a place where she could entertain friends and family, something she was unable to do in her small home. And friends and family are exactly what she considers each and every customer who walks through Gracie's gracious doors.

"I never felt I could entertain in my house because it is really tiny," Judy explains. "So when I retired, I decided to open up a shop of some sort to fill that hostess void. In the beginning, I had no idea it would be a tearoom."

Against all odds, considering her lack of capital and experience, but backed by her faith and the prayers of friends, Judy got a loan, found a location, and opened her tearoom. She named it Gracie's to reflect her belief that it was only through God's grace that she was able to realize her dream. She now operates the tearoom with her partner and cousin Sandy Boswell. Gracie's quickly became the talk of the town, and Judy likes to say, "We don't just serve a cup of tea; we serve a cup of comfort."

How true this is. Once seated, the guest has a choice of teas in tempting flavors like black currant, Darjeeling, Earl Grey, English breakfast, mixed berry, and many more. The tables are adorned with antique cups and saucers in varying patterns, each unique and obviously used with love—the occasional nick or crack only adding to their charm. When the chosen tea arrives in a personal tea-pot, the server pours the first cup through a delicate silver strainer. The pungent aroma of the fresh brew is enough to whisk you away, but the tea party is just beginning.

Out come the teatime accompaniments, a mix of savory and sweet treats that will melt in your mouth. Scones that are at once dense and airy taste even better with a dab of the delicious almond crème or lemon curd. Fresh fruit, Gracie's signature chicken salad tea sandwiches, and crisp baguettes with tomatoes and snipped dill are served, followed by a decadent selection of desserts. Turtle brownies, pound cake drizzled with peach liqueur, and still-warm oatmeal-raisin cookies add the perfect finishing touch.

Judy and Sandy feel their tearoom has become a haven for many of their regulars. Each visitor will find that same sense of comfort at Gracie's. As you tip the cup to drink the last, wonderful drop of tea and savor the last bite of scone, you will feel serenely satisfied and realize that as the tea has warmed the body, the experience has warmed the soul.

Tea for two is wonderful at Gracie's, but special occasions like bridal or baby showers, and children's birthdays can be uniquely celebrated at the tearoom too, and while Gracie's welcomes everyone, reservations are usually required.

ഇറ

Gracie's English Tearoom is located at 1734 Mulberry Street, Montgomery, Alabama. Call 334-240-2444 for reservations. Hours are 10 a.m. to 4 p.m. Tuesday through Saturday.

⤐ RECIPES ⤏

CHICKEN APPLE DUMPLINGS • STRAWBERRY BREAD
• 18 KARAT CAKE

Designed to pair perfectly with loose-leaf tea selections, the tea foods served at Gracie's are beautiful and delicious, with a nice Southern accent.

Savory Chicken Apple Dumplings are given a sweet-tart twist with the addition of Granny Smith apples.

CHICKEN APPLE DUMPLINGS
Makes 8 dumplings

1   (3-ounce) package cream cheese
6   tablespoons butter, melted
2   cups chopped cooked chicken
2   tablespoons milk
$1/4$ teaspoon salt
$1/2$ teaspoon garlic powder
$1/8$ teaspoon ground black pepper
1   large Granny Smith apple or 2 medium apples, chopped
2   (8-ounce) cans refrigerated crescent rolls
Garnish: fresh parsley

1. Preheat oven to 350°. Spray muffin tin with nonstick cooking spray.
2. In large bowl, combine cream cheese and butter. Add chicken, milk, salt, garlic powder, and pepper; mix thoroughly. Stir in apple.
3. Unroll crescent dough, separating into 4 rectangles; press perforations to seal. Roll out each rectangle slightly. Place rectangles into prepared muffin tins to create four corners.
4. Fill each muffin tin with $1/3$ cup cream cheese-chicken mixture. Bake 20 to 25 minutes. Garnish with fresh parsley, if desired.

STRAWBERRY BREAD
Makes 2 loaves

2   (10-ounce) packages frozen strawberries, thawed and undrained
4   eggs
$1^1/_2$ cups vegetable oil
3   cups flour, divided
1   teaspoon baking soda
3   teaspoons cinnamon
1   teaspoon salt
2   cups sugar
1 to $1^1/_4$ cups chopped pecans

1. Preheat oven to 350°. Grease and lightly flour 2 (9x5x3-inch) loaf pans.
2. In medium bowl, combine strawberries with liquid, eggs, and oil. In small bowl, sift together $1^1/_2$ cups flour, baking soda, cinnamon, salt, and sugar; stir into strawberry mixture and blend thoroughly.
3. In small bowl, combine pecans and $1^1/_2$ cups flour. Add pecan mixture to strawberry mixture, stirring to combine thoroughly.
4. Divide batter evenly between prepared loaf pans. Bake 1 hour or until wooden pick inserted near center comes out clean. Cool in pans on wire rack 10 minutes. Remove from pans and cool completely on wire rack.

Note: If top starts to brown before done, place loose 'tent' of foil over loaves.

18 KARAT CAKE
Makes one cake

2   cups all-purpose flour
2   teaspoons baking soda
2   teaspoons cinnamon
$1^1/_2$ teaspoons salt
3   eggs
$^3/_4$ cup vegetable oil
$^3/_4$ cup buttermilk
2   cups sugar
2   teaspoons vanilla extract
1   (8-ounce) can crushed pineapple, drained
2   cups grated carrots
$3^1/_2$ ounces shredded coconut
1   cup chopped walnuts
18 Karat Cake Buttermilk Glaze (recipe follows)
Cream Cheese Frosting (recipe follows)
Garnish: carrot strips (approximately 6 inches), fresh mint

Strawberries, cinnamon, and pecans combine to make this sweet bread. The recipe makes two loaves, so slice it up and send your guests home with this wonderful treat.

1. Preheat oven to 350°. Grease and flour 9x13x2-inch pan.

2. In large bowl, sift together flour, baking soda, cinnamon, and salt. In medium bowl, beat eggs. Add oil, buttermilk, sugar, and vanilla extract. Mix thoroughly.

3. Add pineapple, carrots, coconut, and walnuts to flour mixture. Mix thoroughly and pour into prepared pan.

4. Bake 50-55 minutes or until wooden pick inserted near center comes out clean.

5. Remove cake from oven. Slowly pour 18 Karat Cake Buttermilk Glaze over hot cake. Cool cake in pan until glaze is absorbed, about 1 hour.

6. Spread cake with Cream Cheese Frosting. Garnish with carrot strips, rolled to resemble flowers, and fresh mint sprigs, if desired. Refrigerate until frosting is set.

18 KARAT CAKE BUTTERMILK GLAZE

1	cup sugar
$^1/_2$	teaspoon baking soda
$^1/_2$	cup buttermilk
8	tablespoons butter
1	tablespoon corn syrup
1	teaspoon vanilla extract

1. In medium saucepan, combine sugar, baking soda, buttermilk, butter, and corn syrup. Bring to boil.

2. Cook 5 minutes, stirring constantly.

3. Remove from heat; stir in vanilla extract.

CREAM CHEESE FROSTING

8	tablespoons butter, softened
1	(8-ounce) package cream cheese, softened
1	teaspoon vanilla extract
3	cups confectioners' sugar
1	teaspoon orange juice
1	teaspoon grated orange zest

In large bowl, combine butter and cream cheese. Using electric mixer at medium speed, beat mixture until creamy. Add vanilla extract, confectioners' sugar, orange juice, and orange zest. Mix until smooth.

While there aren't 18 carrots in this traditional Southern cake, the flavor strikes culinary gold. Garnished with carrot strips resembling flowers, these cake morsels taste as good as they look.

THE HERMITAGE HOTEL
Nashville, Tennessee

Having hosted such luminaries as Charlton Heston, Steven Spielberg, and Tallulah Bankhead, as well as six presidents, the Hermitage in Nashville is the place to stay in Music City.

Named after Andrew Jackson's Hermitage estate, The Hermitage Hotel in Nashville serves as an inviting refuge, just as the late general's home did nearly two centuries ago. In 1910, the Hermitage opened as the city's first million-dollar hotel, featuring some of the finest interiors in the area with Italian sienna marble, Russian walnut wall panels, and a gorgeous cut, stained-glass ceiling in the lobby. While the original advertisements boasted fire-proof, noise-proof, and dust-proof rooms, today the hotel is striving for boutique status and offers luxurious amenities in plush surroundings that are the result of a recent $20 million restoration.

The opening of the Hermitage marked the emergence of Nashville as a major Southern city, with the hotel serving as the center of all social activity. Drawing famous politicians, actresses, and singers, the Hermitage has quite a varied and rich history. Over the years, the five-star hotel has hosted not only six presidents, and celebrities such as Greta Garbo, Steven Spielberg, and Oprah Winfrey, but it has also held the longest running hotel musical act with the Francis Craig Orchestra, and served as the headquarters for a major political campaign.

Today, along with the history that practically oozes from its walls, the Hermitage lures guests with its award-winning service and surroundings. Holding both the Mobil Five Star and AAA Five Diamond awards, it is also listed on the National Register of Historic Places.

Following a tradition set forth in the early 1930s, the hotel is still a popular venue for social gatherings of any kind, be it a bridal shower, wedding party, or business meeting. This is due, in part, to the detailed, golden-hued interiors, superb service from the staff, and its renowned restaurant, The Capitol Grille.

And when guests need a break from the bustling glitz of the city, the Hermitage is waiting to provide the perfect retreat, complete with Afternoon Tea. Served Thursday through Sunday starting at 3:00 in the afternoon, the Hermitage provides a full service sit-down tea with a delicious á la carte menu. Reservations are recommended as the word has spread, thanks to delectable treats such as their oft-requested currant scones, Dobosh Cake, and an ever-evolving menu of tea sandwiches. The menu is further complemented with a variety of English teas, truffles, chocolates, and a selection of other sweets.

Just as a gracious hostess leaves no one out, the people behind the scenes at the Hermitage have not forgotten little ones. The concierge provides an entertaining and modern-day etiquette lesson for the little ones, eschewing traditional etiquette advice and instead sharing, for example, that ladies should not, in fact, spread gossip. This upbeat etiquette service culminates in a tea tailored to the students, serving both the purpose of teaching decorum and instilling a love for the ritual of Afternoon Tea.

Having passed the test of time for almost a century, The Hermitage Hotel has certainly set a benchmark for Nashville. Soak up a sense of history and enjoy an afternoon of delightful tea combined with classic Southern hospitality.

ℰᗡᗯ

The Hermitage Hotel is located at 231 Sixth Avenue North, Nashville, Tennessee. Afternoon Tea is available Thursday through Sunday from 3 to 4:30 p.m. Reservations are required, but not limited to guests of the Hermitage. For reservations or more information, call 615-244-3121. www.thehermitagehotel.com.

RECIVES

MASCARPONE HAM TEA SANDWICHES • CURRANT SCONES • DOBOSH CAKE

Reservations are recommended for tea at the Hermitage, and it's easy to see why. The food is delicious. The following recipes are just a sampling of the available delectables for Afternoon Tea.

Salty, sliced ham is sweetly balanced by rich mascarpone cheese laced with honey for a perfect tea sandwich.

MASCARPONE HAM TEA SANDWICHES
Makes 16 tea sandwiches

1/4	cup butter, softened
4	slices rye bread, crusts removed
1/4	cup mascarpone
2	teaspoons honey
4	(1/8-inch-thick) slices rosemary or Virginia-baked ham
1	cup arugula

1. Lightly spread butter on bread slices.
2. In small bowl, combine mascarpone and honey. Spread mixture on bread slices over butter.
3. Top each bread slice with ham slice and arugula.
4. Slice each sandwich into quarters.

CURRANT SCONES
Makes 18 scones

2 1/4	cups all-purpose flour
2	tablespoons sugar
1	teaspoon baking powder
1	teaspoon baking soda
1/8	teaspoon salt
2	tablespoons orange fresh zest
1	tablespoon lemon fresh zest
1/2	cup butter, cold and cubed
1/2	cup dried currants, or dried fruit of choice
1/2	cup buttermilk
1	large egg
1	egg white, slightly beaten
2	tablespoons sparkling sugar or sugar in the raw

1. Preheat oven to 325°. Line a baking sheet with parchment paper.
2. In large bowl, combine flour, sugar, baking powder, baking soda and salt. Stir in orange zest and lemon zest. Using pastry blender, cut in butter until mixture is crumbly. Stir in currants.
3. In small bowl, combine buttermilk and egg. Combine buttermilk mixture and flour mixture, stirring until dough is just combined.
4. On lightly floured surface, roll dough to $1/2$-inch thickness. Using 2-inch round cutter, cut scones. Brush scones with egg white, and dust with sugar.
5. Place on prepared baking sheet; bake 12-14 minutes, or until lightly browned.

DOBOSH CAKE
Makes 1 cake

$3/4$ cup butter
1   cup sugar, divided
7   eggs, separated
1   teaspoon vanilla extract
$1/8$ teaspoon salt
2   tablespoons orange zest
1   tablespoon lemon zest
$1^1/4$ cups sifted cake flour
$2/3$ cup raspberry jam, melted
1   (24-ounce) package rolled fondant
Garnish: fresh raspberries, mint

A derivation of the Austrian Dobos Torte, this recipe for Dobosh Cake uses raspberry jam and fondant instead of the original's chocolate and caramel. This makes the cake lighter and perfectly suited for Afternoon Tea.

1. Preheat oven to 325°. Line 2 (17x12x1-inch) baking pans with parchment paper.
2. In medium bowl and using electric mixer at medium speed, beat together butter and $1/2$ cup sugar until fluffy.
3. In medium bowl, combine egg yolks, vanilla extract, and salt. Add egg mixture to butter mixture in thirds, mixing after each addition. Stir in orange zest and lemon zest.
4. In separate medium bowl and using electric mixer at high speed, beat egg whites to soft peaks. Slowly add $1/2$ cup sugar and beat until stiff peaks form. Gently fold meringue into butter mixture. Fold in flour. Divide mixture and spread in prepared pans. Bake approximately 20 minutes. Remove from pans and cool. Cut layers in four 3x17-inch pieces.
5. Spread thin layer of jam on each layer and stack. Roll fondant to $1/8$-inch thickness to fit top of cake. Trim excess and top cake with fondant.
6. Garnish with fresh raspberries and mint, if desired.

KATHLEEN'S TEA ROOM & DAY SPA
Fletcher, North Carolina

Each room of the 100-year-old house that is home to Kathleen's Tea Room and Spa is a delight to the senses.

Located in the tiny town of Fletcher, about 10 miles from Asheville, Kathleen's Tea Room & Day Spa offers a bustling crowd of regulars and newcomers the comforts of Afternoon Tea combined with the catering services of a spa—including a green tea manicure, a peppermint tea twist body wrap, and a detoxifying green tea Swedish massage. Pamper your body and then pamper your taste buds when you enter Kathleen's Tea Room and peruse the menu of fine teas.

Owner Tami Halliman has a wealth of knowledge of herbs and is a Certified Natural Health Consultant. The Spa staff promises that "The moment you walk through the door, our time is devoted to you. You are our sole purpose, whether you spend an hour or a day with us." And you are pampered to a "tea" when you enter the wonderful establishment.

After a morning of beauty, Afternoon Tea is served, and the real fun begins—sitting down for a spot of tea and a three-tiered tray of treats prepared by the tearoom's chef, Adam Bachmeyer. The care he takes with the food he serves, right down to the homemade crackers served with the soup starters, is simply nothing short of spectacular.

In addition to traditional tiered fare, Adam offers a variety of sandwiches, pastas, and desserts for your enjoyment. As well, for the light appetite or early tea, there is Kathleen's Cream Tea, a personal tray bearing a delicious scone served with Devonshire cream and gingered lemon curd, with fresh fruits and a choice of tea. Another favorite

is the Any-timer Tea Tray, a masterful blend of sandwiches, fruits, crackers and cheeses, and a scone accompanied by curd and cream.

Adam, who works under the tutelage of Tami, is constantly adding to and perfecting the menu, with seasonal offerings such as gingered lemon curd, tea-smoked turkey, ginger lemon straws, grilled apple and sage croissants flavored with goat cheese, and orange-raspberry rum cake.

All the tasty treats are served with a full battery of Harney & Sons tea, including the Ragamuffin blend, created by a tearoom regular—Cynthia Fore, a former non-tea-drinker who, through a series of circumstances, met John Harney and attained his guidance in coming up with the flavorful blend. The Earl Gray-based tea (Cynthia will reveal only this among her top-secret list of ingredients) inspired another of Adam's winning teatime treats—homemade fig pastries, a rustic, Ragamuffin Tea-infused tart that is perfect for a festive tea menu.

Kathleen's is available for practically any engagement and the staff will help you plan accordingly. They offer tea seminars, tea etiquette classes, celebri-teas, Breakfast at "Tea-finnay's," Bible studies, tea pairings, bridal luncheons, bridal showers, baby showers, and birthday parties, among others.

The tearoom is comfortably at home in a 100-year-old house, where each room offers new delights to the senses.

ℰℴℭℛ

Kathleen's Tea Room & Day Spa is located at 188 St. Johns Road, Fletcher, North Carolina. Tearoom hours are Tuesday-Saturday 9:30 a.m. to 3 p.m. Call 828-651-4762 for reservations. www.kathleenstearoom.com

RECISES ❧

After a green tea manicure and a spa treatment, it's time for tea. Kathleen's Tea Room & Day Spa serves up tea food favorites as well as seasonal offerings, all served with pots of piping hot tea.

The chef at Kathleen's incorporates tea in many of the tearoom's signature specialties, producing flavorful treats.

SAVORY CRACKERS
Makes about 20 pieces

1	cup flour
1	teaspoon salt
1	tablespoon chives
1	teaspoon loose-leaf black and caramel tea blend
½	teaspoon paprika
1	teaspoon fresh minced garlic
1	teaspoon fresh minced thyme
2	tablespoons cold butter, cubed
¼	cup water, ice cold

1. Preheat oven to 275°. Grease baking sheet.
2. In work bowl of food processor, combine flour, salt, chives, tea, paprika, garlic, and thyme. Add butter and pulse to combine.
3. With machine running, slowly add water to work bowl until soft ball of dough forms.
4. On lightly floured surface, roll dough very thin. Place on prepared baking sheet; bake 20 minutes. Remove from oven and turn cracker over. Bake additional 20 minutes. Check for crispness.
5. Cool, break into rustic-style pieces, and serve.

Note: For testing purposes, we used Harney & Sons Paris blend.

SAVORY CHEVRE CROSTADA
Makes 10 pastries

1   cup goat cheese, at room temperature
$1/4$ cup chopped chives
Pinch salt
Pinch ground black pepper
1   large egg, beaten
1   cup unbleached all-purpose flour
$1/2$ cup spelt flour or wheat flour
$1^{1/2}$ tablespoons sugar
$1/4$ teaspoon salt
2   teaspoons finely ground flavored black tea
10   tablespoons cold butter, cubed
3   tablespoons water, ice cold
Garnish: chopped chives

This flavorful crostada is perfect with an Assam or even a light Darjeeling. The delicate flavors suit the savory pastry to almost any tea or blend.

1. Preheat oven to 375°. Line baking sheet with parchment paper.
2. In medium bowl, combine goat cheese, chives, salt, pepper, and egg. Mix until creamy.
3. In work bowl of food processor, combine all-purpose flour, spelt flour, sugar, salt, and tea. Add butter and pulse to blend. Slowly add water and pulse until dough forms tightly packed ball. Divide dough into 10 equal balls.
4. On lightly floured surface, roll each dough ball into 4-inch round.
5. Evenly divide goat cheese mixture between rounds.
6. Pinch dough at sides of rounds and fold over onto cheese mixture, about $1/2$-inch toward the center. Repeat this step, working around dough, overlapping each fold. Result should be 3-inch crostada with about two inches of cheese mixture visible.
7. Bake 20 minutes or until golden brown. Garnish with chopped chives, if desired.

RAGAMUFFIN FIG PASTRIES
Makes about 30 pastries

¾ cup strong-brewed Ragamuffin tea blend
2 cups chopped dried figs
½ cup sugar
2 tablespoons fresh orange zest
⅛ cup fresh-squeezed orange juice
¼ teaspoon cinnamon
½ cup butter, softened
1 cup brown sugar
3 large eggs
1 teaspoon vanilla extract
2½ cups all-purpose, non-bleached flour
¼ teaspoon baking soda
½ teaspoon salt
Dash nutmeg
Confectioners' sugar

1. Brew Ragamuffin tea, steeping 3-5 minutes. In medium saucepan, simmer figs, tea, sugar, orange zest, orange juice, and cinnamon until mixture is thick and syrupy. Cool.
2. In medium bowl and using electric mixer at medium speed, beat together butter and brown sugar; add eggs and vanilla extract. In medium bowl, sift flour, baking soda, salt and nutmeg. Add to butter mixture and blend well.
3. On lightly floured surface, knead dough until smooth. Chill dough one hour.
4. Preheat oven to 375°. Lightly grease baking sheet.
5. Roll dough into rectangle and cut into strips about 4-inches wide. Carefully spoon filling in center of each length of dough. Using dough knife, fold over; pinch together and seal at side.
6. With seam side down, cut each length of filled dough into 12 pieces of equal size. Place on prepared baking sheet and bake 15 minutes, or until golden. Cool. Dust with confectioners' sugar.

Ragamuffin Fig Pastries are flavored with a Harney & Sons Blend developed by a patron at Kathleen's.

THE LADIES OF LUCERNE TEA ROOM
St. Louis, Missouri

Owner Adrienne Ritter personally greets each and every guest who enters The Ladies of Lucerne Tea Room.

American tea drinkers owe at least a small debt to St. Louis. During the 1904 World's Fair, the world at large got its first taste of iced tea, thanks to Richard Blechynden, India Tea Commissioner and Director of the East Indian Pavilion. The story goes that Blechynden, also a tea plantation owner, planned to give away piping hot samples of his tea—until the summer heat of St. Louis decreased demand to almost nil. Inspiration struck, however, and the tea vendor added ice to his beverage. Business was booming in no time, and though already consumed to a limited degree in other parts of the country, iced tea became a hit after the 1904 exposition ended.

Today, the tea experience is a growing concept in St. Louis, a city that has embraced the most popular hot beverage on the globe—albeit in a manner that is entirely consistent with the spirit of St. Louis.

For those craving a traditional, classic service, The Ladies of Lucerne Tea Room is an equally lovely choice. Located just west of St. Louis proper in Ballwin, Missouri, The Ladies of Lucerne is snugly housed in the Great Hall of the historic Barn at Lucerne, a renovated European-style structure that was once part of a dairy farm.

The Ladies of Lucerne Tea Room, open since 2003, is equal parts upscale gift shop, tearoom, and dining destination for ladies who lunch. And while gender friendly to all, the curve is unmistakably feminine—from the eye-catching décor to the charming trinkets, teapots, and more for sale in the gift shop.

The most feminine aspect of The Ladies of Lucerne, however, is owner Adrianne Ritter—both in her elegant appearance and her warm demeanor.

"There's a lot going on in the world that's negative. People need to be nurtured," says Adrianne, an Alabama native whose drawl becomes charmingly more pronounced when speaking with fellow Southerners. "I think this (business) is in my nature—part sounding board and part hostess."

Adrianne, who is assisted by a staff of 20 but who makes it a point to greet her guests personally, says the reward for her is meeting newcomers and mingling with regulars, ("There's a story at every table," is her favorite saying) and also using the tearoom as a tool to help other women.

Lunch is served daily at The Ladies of Lucerne Tea Room, while full, formal teas are served by reservation only on Saturdays. In addition, the tearoom boasts a full calendar of special tea-related events, many of them staged to raise money for women's causes, such as a recent luncheon and fashion show in which all the models were breast cancer survivors. Other events or "JFFs," (just-for-fun) tea parties include such events as Afternoon Tea with Agatha Christie, A Mad Hatter's

Tea Party, and regular Afternoon Tea and etiquette programs for little ones (for which Brownies and Girl Scouts can earn etiquette merit badges).

In addition to endless pots of fresh premium Harney & Sons tea and tisanes, hot fresh scones, real Devonshire cream, and hand-whipped lemon curd, guests at The Ladies of Lucerne can also expect a heavenly selections of finger sandwiches (the grilled chicken salad is a must), pastries, and tempting desserts—all prepared by the tearoom's kitchen staff under the direction of the owner. It is a point of pride for Adrianne that her guests savor each bite and linger as long as they like at each table.

"I love that I've created an atmosphere that nurtures women," Adrianne says. "Women are always the care-takers and I think it's important that we attend to those who care for others."

Perhaps it is a lingering feeling left behind by the pioneers of old, or maybe it's simply the friendliness of the people who live there, but St. Louis is indeed a city that invites exploration.

"It's the complete destination—we have a little bit of everything, we have history, we have great attractions, and wonderful dining—all wrapped up in warm Midwestern hospitality," tourism guide Mary Hendron says. "We are a city filled with surprises."

The Ladies of Lucerne Tea Room is located in West County at 930 Kehrs Mill Road, and can be reached at 636-227-7300. Lunch is served in the tearoom from 11:00 – 2:00 Tuesday through Friday (reservations recommended). Afternoon Tea is served on Saturdays from 12:00 – 3:00 (reservations required). www.ladiesoflucerne.com

~ RECIPES ~

ITALIAN CHEESE AND BROCCOLI QUICHE • LEMON BLUEBERRY SCONES
• WHITE CHOCOLATE RASPBERRY BARS

The food offered at The Ladies of Lucerne, all prepared under the direction of owner, Adrienne Ritter, is meant to be savored.

In addition to adding hearty flavor to teatime, this savory quiche also pairs nicely with a fresh green salad for a light lunch.

ITALIAN CHEESE AND BROCCOLI QUICHE
Makes 8 servings

1   (9-inch) deep dish pie crust
1   cup shredded Italian 4-cheese blend
1   cup frozen chopped broccoli, thawed
$\frac{1}{2}$ cup chopped red bell pepper
$\frac{1}{3}$ cup chopped fully cooked bacon
4   large eggs
$1\frac{1}{4}$ cups half-and-half
$\frac{1}{2}$ teaspoon salt
$\frac{1}{4}$ teaspoon ground black pepper
$\frac{1}{4}$ teaspoon nutmeg

1. Preheat oven to 375°.
2. Bake pie crust 15 minutes.
3. Sprinkle half of cheese over baked crust. Layer broccoli, bell pepper, bacon, and remaining cheese in pie shell.
4. In medium bowl, beat together eggs, half-and-half, salt, pepper, and nutmeg. Pour over broccoli mixture.
5. Bake 25-30 minutes or until set. Remove from oven and cool 30 minutes before serving.

LEMON BLUEBERRY SCONES
Makes 16 scones

$2\frac{1}{2}$ cups all-purpose flour
$1\frac{1}{2}$ tablespoons baking powder
$\frac{1}{3}$ cup sugar
1   tablespoon fresh lemon zest
$\frac{1}{2}$ cup dried blueberries
$\frac{1}{3}$ cup butter, melted
$\frac{3}{4}$ cup heavy cream

84

1. Preheat oven to 400°. Line baking sheet with parchment paper.

2. In medium bowl, combine flour, baking powder, sugar, lemon zest, and blueberries. Form well in center; add butter and cream. Mix together until dough forms a soft ball.

3. On lightly floured surface, roll dough into ³/₄-inch thickness. Using 2-inch round cutter, cut scones. Arrange about 1 inch apart on prepared baking sheet. Bake 12-15 minutes, or until golden brown.

Note: Dough may be chilled overnight. Let stand at room temperature for 30 minutes and prepare as recommended.

WHITE CHOCOLATE RASPBERRY BARS
Makes 12 bars

¹/₂	cup butter
1	(12-ounce) package vanilla milk morsels or 2 (6-ounce) packages white baking bars, chopped and divided
2	large eggs
¹/₂	cup granulated sugar
1	cup all-purpose flour
¹/₂	teaspoon salt
1	teaspoon amaretto liqueur or almond extract
¹/₂	cup raspberry jam
¹/₄	cup sliced almonds, toasted

Garnish: fresh raspberries

1. Preheat oven to 325°. Grease and flour 9-inch square pan.

2. In small saucepan over low heat, melt butter. Add 1 cup vanilla milk morsels. Let stand; do not stir.

3. In large bowl and using electric mixer at high speed, beat eggs until foamy. Gradually add sugar, beating until lemon-colored. Stir in butter mixture. Add flour, salt and amaretto; mix at low speed until just combined. Spread half of batter (about 1 cup) in pan. Bake 10-15 minutes, or until golden brown.

4. In small saucepan over low heat, melt jam. Spread evenly over warm, partially baked crust.

5. Stir 1 cup vanilla milk morsels into remaining batter. Gently spoon teaspoonfuls of remaining batter over jam. (Some jam may show through batter.) Sprinkle with almonds.

6. Return to oven; bake additional 25 to 30 minutes or until wooden pick inserted near center comes out clean. Cool completely. Cut into bars. Garnish serving plate or individual bars with fresh raspberries, if desired.

Raspberries, slivered almonds, and white chocolate combine to make a dessert bar that won't last long around the house.

MARTIN HOUSE INN
Nantucket, Massachusetts

Martin House Inn, built in 1803 as a family residence, is a stately relic of whaling's heyday on Nantucket Island.

Just 30 miles off the coast of Massachusetts, cradled in the waters of the Atlantic, is an island paradise. For those fortunate to live on Nantucket, and those who come to vacation, it is truly a bit of heaven on earth.

Our travel destination, Martin House Inn, built in 1803 by a sea captain for his bride, is among the many great houses on the island constructed during the whaling heyday. Located on Centre Street, mere minutes by foot from the wharf where ferries deposit eager visitors, Martin House Inn is a perfect blend of contemporary convenience and tranquil accommodations. The comfortable house offers luxuries such as four-poster and canopy beds dressed in designer linens, fireplaces, and seating areas within the bedrooms. Impressive artwork from local artists such as Paul Galschneider, Paul Arsenault, and others create an inviting center from which visitors can strike out to see the island.

After a day of sightseeing, looking for shells on the beach, or taking a painting or basket-weaving class, guests at Martin House Inn head back to enjoy the pleasures of Afternoon Tea, prepared by Innkeeper Lee Sylva. With her experience of almost 30 years in food service, she brings a sense of ease in her approach to the preparation of tea foods.

On cold or blustery days, guests gather fireside in the cozy living room, or at the expansive dining room table to share the tea delicacies, family style. Fair weather finds the tea service located on the veranda, where guests can enjoy the beautiful and tasty tea foods, with cups of steaming tea, while savoring the salt-laden sea air.

Savories and sweets vary according to season, and the tiered tray may include such custom creations as Lee's arugula butter with cucumber sandwich or delicate smoked salmon tea sandwiches, with lemon squares or chocolate chunk orange cake.

"Scones vary from day to day. I like to make lemon scones and cranberry scones. The Inn's pantry is my inspiration," says the innkeeper. Devonshire cream and jam accompany the scones.

Take note of the charming white china used for serving tea at the Inn. Nantucket resident George Davis, inspired by the traditional lightship baskets that for years have been synonymous with the island, crafted the china pattern, which today is one of Wedgwood's most popular patterns.

Be prepared to enjoy the relaxed pace of life on the island. Strolling the streets that wind among cottages and mansions, admiring the profusion of flowers that bloom with abandon, savoring the blue sky and mild temperatures are favored ways of getting acquainted with Nantucket. Walking is the preferred means of transportation in town, though bicycles and taxis are available for rent.

The boomerang-shaped spit of land that is historic Nantucket Island is little changed since the glory days of whaling more than 400 years ago. With unspoiled beaches, miles of land preserved from development, streets free of neon signs and traffic lights, Nantucket is a dream destination.

Martin House Inn is located at 61 Centre Street, Nantucket, Massachusetts. To book a stay, call Lee Sylva at 508-228-0678. www.martinhouseinn.com

⟨RECIPES⟩

WILD MUSHROOM VOL-AU-VENT • TOASTED COCONUT AND MANGO SCONES
• BERRY TARTS WITH RICOTTA CREAM

Using the Inn's pantry as inspiration, Lee Sylva creates delightful teatime treats that reflect the seasons.

Vol-au-vent is a puff pastry shell that resembles a pot with a lid. The hearty wild mushroom filling is perfect with tea, and the dish is impressive in its presentation.

WILD MUSHROOM VOL-AU-VENT
Makes 6 pastries

1	(10-ounce) package frozen puff pastry shells
1	(1-ounce) package dried wild mushrooms (such as porcini or morels)
1	pound white button mushrooms
3	tablespoons unsalted butter
2	large shallots
2	tablespoons chopped fresh tarragon or 2 tablespoons dried

1 to 2 teaspoons fresh lemon juice
$1/2$ cup heavy cream
$1/8$ teaspoon grated fresh nutmeg
1 tablespoon chopped flat leaf parsley
$1/8$ teaspoon salt
$1/8$ teaspoon freshly ground black pepper
Garnish: chopped parsley

1. Following package directions, bake puff pastry shells; set aside.
2. In small bowl, cover dried wild mushrooms with boiling water. Soak 30 minutes.
3. Using cheesecloth or fine sieve, strain mushrooms, reserving liquid. In medium saucepan over medium heat, simmer mushroom liquid until reduced to about 2 tablespoons.
4. Combine button mushrooms with wild mushrooms; chop.
5. In large skillet over medium-low heat, melt butter. Add shallots and cook 1 minute. Add mushrooms, mushroom liquid, and tarragon; cook, stirring frequently, until all liquid has evaporated. Add lemon juice. Stir in cream and nutmeg; simmer over low heat, stirring frequently, 15 minutes, or until cream is thoroughly absorbed by mushrooms. Add chopped parsley, salt, and pepper. Keep warm.
6. Spoon filling into puff pastry shells. Garnish with parsley, if desired. Serve warm.

TOASTED COCONUT AND MANGO SCONES
Makes about 36 scones

1   cup sugar
4   cups all-purpose flour
2   teaspoons baking powder
$1/2$ teaspoon baking soda
$1/4$ teaspoon salt
1   cup unsalted butter, cubed
1   cup sweetened, shredded coconut, toasted
1   cup dried mango, diced
2   cups heavy cream

1. Preheat oven to 400°. Line baking sheet with parchment paper.
2. In large bowl, sift together sugar, flour, baking powder, baking soda, and salt. Using pastry blender, cut in butter until crumbly. Stir in coconut and mango.
3. Add cream and mix until crumbly ball forms. On lightly floured surface, knead lightly. Roll into 8x11-inch rectangle. Fold dough into thirds lengthwise. Turn dough and roll and fold. Repeat three times. Roll into rectangle and cut in half lengthwise. Using 3-inch floured triangle-shaped cutter, cut scones.
4. Place scones on prepared baking sheet. Bake on middle rack 15-20 minutes, or until edges are golden brown and wooden pick inserted in center comes out clean. Place on wire racks and cover with linen towels. Cool completely.

The tropical flavors of coconut and mango give these scones an exotic taste.

BERRY TARTS WITH RICOTTA CREAM
Makes 10 tarts

8   tablespoons unsalted butter, cubed
$1/2$ cup sugar
$1^1/2$ cups all-purpose flour
$1/8$ teaspoon salt
1   egg yolk
2   tablespoons heavy cream
Ricotta Cream (recipe follows)

1   pint strawberries, thinly sliced
1   pint blueberries
1   pint raspberries
1   pint blackberries

1. In work bowl of food processor, combine butter and sugar; pulse 15 times, or until mixture is well combined. Add flour and salt; pulse 15 times, or until mixture is crumbly.
2. In small bowl, combine egg yolk and cream. Add to butter mixture and pulse until just incorporated. Dough will be crumbly.
3. Place in plastic bag and shape into round form until dough holds together. Remove from bag and knead until dough becomes one smooth round. Flatten into one 6-inch disk. Wrap and refrigerate 30 minutes.
4. Preheat oven to 350°.
5. Position dough between lightly floured sheets of plastic wrap; roll to $1/16$-inch-thick circle. Remove top piece of plastic wrap and cut dough into 5-inch circles. Line each 4-inch tart pan with dough round. Place parchment rounds on top of dough in pans. Place pie weights or dried beans over parchment paper, making sure to fill to cover sides.
6. Bake 6 minutes. Remove shells from oven. Remove weights or beans from tart pans; prick each with fork, and continue baking 6 minutes, or until lightly browned. (If centers rise during baking, press down.) Cool and remove from pans.
7. Spoon layer of Ricotta Cream into cooled tart shells. Arrange berries as desired on top.

RICOTTA CREAM
Makes 2 cups

2   cups whole milk ricotta cheese
$1/4$ cup confectioners' sugar
3   tablespoons almond liqueur or orange cognac

Drain excess liquid from ricotta. In work bowl of food processor, pulse until smooth. Add confectioners' sugar and liqueur; blend well.

The surprise ingredient in these flavorful summery tarts is ricotta cheese. Sweetened with confectioners' sugar and a bit of liqueur for flavor, the creamy filling is a delectable base for a topping of naturally sweet berries.

MISS MABLE'S TEAROOM
Dickson, Tennessee

Mable is an acronym for Mothers Always Bring a Loving Experience, and you'll find that familial warmth at Miss Mable's.

Miss Mable's is the kind of place that most little girls (and grown-up ones too) conjure up in daydreams. The tearoom is a sort of secret garden to share with one's girlfriends, play dress-up, sip tea, and shop. And that's exactly what owner Fay Davidson had in mind when she opened Miss Mable's Tearoom.

In every room, fresh flowers peek out of vases while crisply pressed linens are tucked and folded at each place setting. Lamplight softens the few corners untouched by sunlight, while soothing music plays in the background. Vintage hats cover nearly every wall in the house, and dressy stoles wait on the backs of chairs for a pair of shoulders to warm. Jewelry, handbags, perfumes, soaps, housewares, and fine china for sale fill the rooms, both upstairs and downstairs.

"My businesses are named after women," says Fay, who also owns a children's tearoom in town named Mrs. Potts. "Miss Mable's stands for 'Mothers Always Bring a Loving Experience.' My own mother and grandmother were great women in my life. They were comforting and loving, and they believed in me, no matter what. They were poised and graceful and Southern and hospitable." Fay adds that both her love of teatime and the idea to open a tearoom grew out of her experiences with beloved women in her life.

Fay Davidson also owns and operates Mrs. Pott's, a tearoom especially for children. At Mrs. Pott's, girls can have a Cinderella-themed birthday party, complete with a magician and a horse-drawn coach.

Fay learned about the comfort and pleasures of tea at her grandmother's side. After her grandfather died, Fay volunteered to live with her grandmother for a year to soothe her sudden and painful loneliness. Though longing for her own mother, Fay remembers sharing solace and serenity with her grandmother—over cups of tea.

"My grandmother was involved with ladies' clubs and socials and church functions. She entertained a lot, especially for other women," Fay says. Doing the same thing for her fellow femmes, on a professional basis, became a wish in the back of Fay's mind. The idea simmered for years, she says, before taking shape—with a little help from her daughter.

"Jennifer and I went to Washington, to Dorothea Johnson's Protocol School of Washington, to take etiquette classes. Initially, we did that mainly to have a mother-daughter bond," she says. Today, that experience is put to practice in the family-operated tearoom.

Miss Mable's is truly a family affair. Fay's husband Mark is a constant in the tearoom, ready to lend a hand when it's needed. Daughter Jennifer helps run the day-to-day business and serves as her mother's co-hostess, while son-in-law Chuck Jones serves as the chef and mastermind behind such offerings as Scrooge's Pumpkin Pie and tea sandwiches made of Boursin cheese blended with mulled spices.

The foods change monthly at Miss Mable's, to complement the themed teas Fay dreams up, like Anne of Green Gables Tea or 12 Teas of Christmas. And though she might occasionally ask Chuck to "frou-frou it up a little bit," Fay says the fit is a good one.

Fay says being surrounded by her family each day at work is, to her, a natural extension of the hospitably Southern and profoundly feminine experience she wants to provide to each and every one of her tearoom customers.

"I have found that even if you're home during the day, you have to learn how to take 30 minutes just for you," she says. "Taking that second breath is important; I wanted that for women, for the caretakers. We need to remember to take care of ourselves too, and take a few minutes to rejuvenate, just for our own peace of mind."

ೞಐ

Miss Mable's Tearoom is located at 301 West College St., Dickson, Tennessee. Luncheon Tea or Afternoon Tea is served from 11:00 a.m. to 2:00 p.m., Tuesday through Saturday. Royal High Tea is served from 5:30 p.m. to 8:00 p.m., Friday and Saturday. For reservations, call 615-441-6658.

RECIPES

MAMMY'S COUNTRY HAM AND TOMATO TARTLET • HAZELNUT SCONES • MISS MABLE'S COOKIE JAR TEA CAKES

At Miss Mables, TEA stands for Taste, Elegance, and Authenticity. You'll find each of those elements in the lovely tea foods they serve.

Country Ham and Tomato Tartlets are perfect for Afternoon Tea. The Cream Cheese Pastry dough can be mixed in a minute. Though small, they are hearty.

MAMMY'S COUNTRY HAM AND TOMATO TARTLET

Makes 24 tartlets

Cream Cheese Pastry (recipe follows)
2 large eggs
1 cup half-and-half
1/2 teaspoon salt
1/3 teaspoon ground black pepper
3/4 cup grated Cheddar cheese
1/2 cup country ham, finely chopped
1/2 cup Roma tomatoes, finely chopped
2 tablespoons finely chopped fresh chives

1. Preheat oven to 350°. Lightly coat mini-muffin tins with cooking spray.
2. On lightly floured surface, roll Cream Cheese Pastry dough to 1/8-inch-thickness. Using 2-inch cutter, cut pastry. Place pastry rounds in wells of prepared mini-muffin tins.
3. In large bowl, whisk together eggs, half-and-half, salt, and pepper.
4. Sprinkle cheese, ham, and tomatoes in pastry shells.
5. Cover with egg mixture and sprinkle with chives.
6. Bake 40-45 minutes, or until golden brown.

CREAM CHEESE PASTRY

1 (3-ounce) package cream cheese, softened
1/2 cup margarine, softened
1 cup flour

In medium bowl and using electric mixer at medium speed, combine cream cheese and butter; blend in flour. Shape into ball. Refrigerate 4-5 hours.

HAZELNUT SCONES
Makes 12 scones

2½ cups all-purpose flour
1   tablespoon baking powder
½   teaspoon salt
⅓   cup firmly packed brown sugar
½   cup butter
½   cup hazelnuts, chopped
½   cup buttermilk
1   large egg, slightly beaten
2   tablespoons heavy cream
2   tablespoons sugar

1. Preheat oven to 400°. Lightly grease baking sheet.
2. In large bowl, sift together flour, baking powder, salt, and brown sugar. Using pastry blender, cut in butter until mixture is crumbly. Add hazelnuts.
3. In small bowl, whisk together buttermilk and egg. Add buttermilk mixture to flour mixture, stirring just until dry ingredients are moistened.
4. On lightly floured surface, roll dough to ½-inch thickness. Using floured heart-shaped cutter, cut scones and place on prepared baking sheet.
5. Brush with cream and sprinkle with sugar. Bake 12-15 minutes, or until golden brown.

MISS MABLE'S COOKIE JAR TEA CAKES
Makes 24 tea cakes

⅔   cup solid shortening
¾   cup sugar
1   large egg
½   teaspoon vanilla extract
½   teaspoon salt
2   cups sifted flour
1½   teaspoons baking powder
2   tablespoons milk
Confectioners' sugar

1. Preheat oven to 375°. Lightly grease baking sheet.
2. Using electric mixer at medium speed, cream shortening and sugar. Add egg; beat mixture until light and creamy. Add vanilla extract.
3. Sift together salt, flour, and baking powder. Add flour mixture to shortening mixture alternately with milk, beating well to combine.
4. Divide dough in half; cover tightly with plastic wrap. Refrigerate 1 hour.
5. On lightly floured surface, roll dough to approximately ⅛-inch thickness; cut in desired shapes and place on prepared cookie sheet.
6. Bake 10 minutes, or until golden brown. Remove from oven. Dust with confectioners' sugar.

MISS ROSEMARIE'S SPECIAL TEAS
Birmingham, Alabama

Rosemarie Kramer welcomes guests with a daily tea tasting. She named her tearoom Special Teas because in her words, "people are special and deserve to be treated so."

In a shopping center not far from Birmingham's busy Highway 280, a comfortable tea salon is the last thing anyone would expect. With its golden interiors and soft piano music, Miss Rosemarie's Special Teas offers a unique and relaxing European-style tea experience.

Warmly welcoming her guests with a daily tea tasting, owner Rosemarie Kramer sets the tone for a lovely visit. "I wanted to provide people with a haven. Somewhere to come in, take a deep breath and relax and enjoy," says Rosemarie. The smell of the daily lunch special and scones baking carries diners to lace-covered tables with tea sets complemented by flowers in a silver mint-julep cup.

Although this is her first venture into the restaurant world, Rosemarie is a skilled and gracious hostess who knows a thing or two about tea. As a little girl, she watched her mother give countless teas and card parties for her friends in Michigan, which led Rosemarie to a love of entertaining and cooking for friends and family. Ultimately, it was an Atlanta decorator who instilled her appreciation for tea. He taught the "art of taking tea" and told his students to treat themselves, to use their good china every day, and to enjoy it. "He really opened my eyes to a whole new world. We went to Europe experiencing tea all over, and now I even love traveling," says Rosemarie.

She holds two certificates from the World Tea Expo, meaning she knows both how to enjoy the beverage and how to explain the science behind it. In fact, Rosemarie offers lectures on topics ranging from the history of tea to how to brew a perfect pot, for anyone interested.

While her personal tea rituals have been taken over by all day tea sipping and pouring, she has no doubt passed the practice on to others through example. "It's just something I've always done. I like to treat people specially, because people are special. That's actually why we named our place 'Special Teas,'" says Rosemarie.

Even customers who come in without reservations during the busiest part of the day are treated with care. Rearranging tables, sliding seats down the tea bar, and still making sure each table has a complete tea set are just a few of the ways customers become guests at Miss Rosemarie's.

Reservations are becoming the norm not only because of her graciousness, but also because of the food. Traditional tea fare—complete with homemade scones and tiny tea sandwiches—is available, as well as daily lunch specials such as the ever-popular crab cakes, and shrimp and grits. Her menu has received rave reviews from men and women alike.

Rosemarie attributes the number of new and repeat guests to the great European, comfortable, and not-too-cutesy ambience of her tea salon. "My favorite thing is to have ladies, and especially men, come in who give the impression that they don't want to be here, and they leave loving it, telling me they will be bringing friends back," says Rosemarie, "You can literally watch them relax."

Miss Rosemarie's Special Teas is located at 5299 Valleydale Road, Birmingham, Alabama. Tea is served Tuesday through Friday 11 a.m. to 4 p.m., and Saturday 11 a.m. to 2 p.m. For reservations, call 205-980-8335.

❧ RECIPES ☙

CREAM OF GINGER CARROT SOUP • CARAMELIZED PEAR, BLUE CHEESE, AND ROASTED WALNUT QUICHE • APPLE BUTTER MINI TARTS

Miss Rosemarie's savories and sweets have received rave reviews from women and men who frequent her teahouse. The soup and quiche pair nicely for lunch, and the apple butter tarts are to be sweetly savored with your favorite infusion.

CREAM OF GINGER CARROT SOUP
Makes 6-8 servings

2   pounds carrots, peeled and chopped
$\frac{1}{8}$ to $\frac{1}{4}$ cup minced ginger
4   cups chicken broth
2   cups heavy cream
Salt
Garnish: shredded carrots, fresh parsley

1. In large saucepan, combine carrots, ginger and chicken broth. Bring to boil over medium heat and cook 30 to 40 minutes. Remove from heat.
2. Place carrot mixture in work bowl of food processor. Puree until mixture is smooth. Add cream and salt to taste. Garnish with shredded carrots and fresh parsley, if desired. Serve immediately.

Cream of Ginger Carrot Soup is one of Miss Rosemarie's favorite recipes. The ginger adds a hint of spice, which contrasts nicely with the sweetness of the carrots. Freeze unused soup in a zip-top bag and serve within three months.

CARAMELIZED PEAR, BLUE CHEESE, AND ROASTED WALNUT QUICHE
Makes 6-8 servings

2 fresh pears
¼ cup walnuts, chopped
5 eggs
1 cup heavy cream
½ teaspoon salt
¼ teaspoon ground black pepper
¼ cup blue cheese, crumbled
1 (9-inch) deep dish pie crust
Garnish: blue cheese crumbles

1. Preheat oven to 350°. Line baking sheet with parchment paper.
2. Peel and cut pears into ⅛-inch-thick slices. Place on prepared baking sheet. Bake 10-12 minutes, or until lightly browned.
3. Spread layer of walnuts on separate baking sheet and bake 5-10 minutes, being careful not to burn.
4. In medium bowl and using electric mixer at medium speed, combine eggs, cream, salt, and pepper and mix 1-2 minutes, or until pale yellow in color.
5. Layer pears, blue cheese, and walnuts on bottom of pie crust. Pour egg mixture over layers to cover. Bake 45 minutes, or until center is set. Garnish with blue cheese crumbles, if desired.

APPLE BUTTER MINI TARTS
Makes 24 mini tarts

1 (8-ounce) package cream cheese
¼ cup plus 2 tablespoons apple butter
24 frozen mini phyllo shells, thawed
Toasted chopped pecans

1. In small bowl, combine cream cheese and ¼ cup apple butter. Mix until smooth and creamy.
2. Pipe cream cheese mixture into phyllo shells and top each tart with ¼ teaspoon of apple butter. Sprinkle with pecans. Refrigerate until ready to serve.

Caramelized pears and blue cheese combine to make a quiche that guests of Miss Rosemarie's request time and again. The dish can be served warm or at room temperature.

THE RITTENHOUSE HOTEL
Philadelphia, Pennsylvania

The Mary Cassatt Tea Room not only takes its name from the painter, but also utilizes the colors of her palette in everything from the décor to the food.

Nestled in a nook of The Rittenhouse Hotel's elegant lobby, the Mary Cassatt Tea Room and Garden offers not only soothing afternoon respite for the weary traveler, but also a sumptuous experience for tea lovers.

Seatings for the classic English-style service are available daily from 2 until 5 p.m. in what is arguably one of the most tranquil spots in the bustling City of Brotherly Love.

Named for Impressionist painter Mary Cassatt—an artist who studied and honed her craft at the Pennsylvania Academy of Fine Arts in Philadelphia—the tearoom has not only adopted the nineteenth-century painter's name, but her delicate sense of aesthetic as well. Appointed in soft floral shades of sunny yellow, rose, pale blue, and cream, The Rittenhouse offers comfortable indoor seating for guests, as well as a soothing outdoor sanctuary in the tearoom's private garden.

Outdoors or in, the tea salon's raison d'etre is, of course, the tea. Served in fine bone china teapots and cups, the salon features a selection of about a dozen Rittenhouse Specialty Blend teas, many of them organic. Along with such timeless infusions as Earl Grey, English Breakfast, and estate Darjeeling, the hotel also offers several delicious blends for the tea lover with a more adventurous palate. Black tea blends such as vanilla bean, pear caramel and Bombay chai are perfect picks

for colder months, while the green tea tropical blend is ideal for warmer months, boasting fruity notes of guava, pineapple, and strawberry.

A three-tiered tray brimming with tea foods that are classically continental in style and presentation accompanies each warming, fragrant pot of tea. The salon's signature Queen Victoria Tea includes a quartet of tea sandwiches and sweets, and freshly baked currant scones with strawberry preserves, lemon curd, and Devonshire cream. Tea pastries, sandwiches, and scones may also be ordered á la carte.

Menu items vary with the season and include a mix of teatime standards, such as egg salad and chives, as well as nouveau classics, such as grilled vegetable Napoleons, tarragon shrimp with fennel frond and Dijonnaise, or perhaps prosciutto with shaved Romano cheese and rocket greens. On the sweets tray, guests are sure to discover such gems as lemon diamonds, profiteroles, or hand-dipped bonbons prepared in-house in the hotel kitchen's chocolate enrobing room.

For parties of 15 or more—ideal for wedding parties, birthdays or showers—the Mary Cassatt Tea Room and Garden also offers a catered tea that includes butlered hors d'ouevres served warm, a table presentation of five tea sandwiches, a selection of sweets, and tea breads. Upon request, soup, fruit, or champagne starters may also be added.

ଽଠଙ୍

The Mary Cassatt Tea Room and Garden is located at The Rittenhouse Hotel, 2210 West Rittenhouse Square, Philadelphia, Pennsylvania. Tea service is available every day from 2 p.m. to 5 p.m. Reservations are required. Call 800-635-1042 or 215-546-9000. www.rittenhousehotel.com

 RECIPES

EGG SALAD SANDWICHES • CURRANT SCONES
• LEMON CREAM WITH CHOCOLATE

The Mary Cassatt Tea Room offers traditional tea fare served in elegant surroundings. Seating in the outdoor garden is also available.

Finely chopped fresh parsley turns a tasty sandwich into a work of art, worthy of the tearoom's namesake.

EGG SALAD SANDWICHES
Makes 48 sandwiches

4   large eggs
4   tablespoons mayonnaise
1   teaspoon Dijon mustard
$\frac{1}{4}$ teaspoon salt
$\frac{1}{8}$ teaspoon ground black pepper
24   slices white bread, crusts removed
Salted butter, at room temperature
Chopped parsley

1. In medium saucepan, place eggs and cover with cold water. Bring to boil and cook 10 minutes. Drain and rinse under cold water. Peel eggs.
2. In medium bowl, combine mayonnaise and mustard. Chop eggs and stir into mixture. Add salt and pepper.
3. Spread egg salad over 12 slices bread; top with remaining bread slices. Cut each sandwich into four pieces. Butter edges of cut sides; dip in chopped parsley.

These sandwiches are the perfect summertime tea fare. Put several in a picnic basket, fill a carafe with hot water, and invite your friends to a local park for a relaxing tea under the trees.

CURRANT SCONES
Makes 12 scones

$\frac{1}{2}$ cup unsalted butter
2 cups all purpose flour
$\frac{1}{4}$ cup whole buttermilk
1 large egg
$\frac{1}{2}$ teaspoon salt
$\frac{1}{2}$ tablespoon baking powder
1 tablespoon sugar
$\frac{1}{2}$ cup dried currants

1. Preheat oven to 350°. Line baking sheet with parchment paper.
2. Using pastry blender, cut butter into flour. Refrigerate 1 hour.
3. In small bowl, combine buttermilk, egg, and salt. Remove flour mixture from refrigerator; stir in baking powder and sugar. Add currants to mixture, stirring until incorporated.
4. Combine buttermilk mixture with flour mixture; stirring just until moistened.
5. On lightly floured surface, roll or pat dough to 1-inch thickness. Using 2-inch round cutter, cut scones. Place scones on prepared baking sheet and bake 14-16 minutes.

LEMON CREAM WITH CHOCOLATE
Makes 3 cups

1 cup heavy cream
$\frac{1}{2}$ cup sugar
$\frac{1}{4}$ cup lemon juice
3 large eggs
2 tablespoons chocolate, shaved
Garnish: shaved chocolate

The pairing of chocolate with lemon results in a refreshing taste treat.

112

1. In medium bowl, and using electric mixer at high speed, beat cream until soft peaks form. Refrigerate.
2. In medium saucepan, combine sugar, lemon juice, and eggs. Cook over medium heat, whisking constantly, 3 minutes, or until slightly thickened. Cool over ice bath.
3. Fold lemon mixture and whipped cream together gently until combined. Fold chocolate shavings into mixture; pour into small ramekins.
4. Garnish with shaved chocolate, if desired. Chill before serving.

WILLARD INTERCONTINENTAL
Washington, D.C.

The attentive staff of the Willard InterContinental ensures that you have a tea experience unparalleled in the District of Columbia.

The Willard InterContinental hotel is a Washington landmark. And, like most landmarks in the Capitol city, the Willard has its share of history. The hotel's motto is "The Residence of Presidents," and short of the White House, the Willard is the finest place to stay in metropolitan D.C. The Willard has hosted, either as an overnight guest or as a guest at a social function, every president since Zachary Taylor in 1850.

The classic Afternoon Tea at the Willard provides guests with premium seating at elegantly appointed tables set in the hotel's Peacock Alley—one of Washington's prime locations to "stroll, strut, see and be seen." Peacock Alley has always been known as a dramatic corridor, connecting the Pennsylvania Avenue entrance with the F street entrance. In the past, the debutantes of Washington would walk up and down the alley in their best dresses. This strutting resembled the strut of peacocks, hence the alley's name.

The Willard's tea menu changes seasonally. During the Christmas holidays, a special holiday tea blend is added, along with Pumpkin and Cranberry Scones, Roast Christmas Goose and Chestnut Sandwiches, and Petite Buche de Noel. Live music from a harpist or a pianist ensures that guests enjoy a truly elegant experience. And in the spring, the season of the Cherry Blossom Festival, the Willard offers a Cherry Blossom Tea, which features a cherry infused brew, sun-dried cherries drenched in Belgian chocolate, and Fresh Cherry Scones. The hotel also has a special Mother's Day Tea. Savories are the most popular items on the menu until Christmas, when the desire for sweets overtakes the dining crowd.

When Miss America Pageant finalists were invited to Afternoon Tea, it was the stately Willard InterContinental that hosted the gathering of hopefuls.

Since its inception in March of 2005, Afternoon Tea at the Willard has become the place to enjoy the finest blends. Servers at the Willard are trained throughout the year with their tea provider, Mighty Leaf. Tableside service from the cherry-wood finished tea cart allows the Willard tea servers to draw guests' specified aromatic right at their table.

The Willard has introduced its own tea, a hand-selected blend of green and oolong teas, which makes the distinct flavor profile exclusive to the hotel. Guests can enjoy it at Afternoon Tea, or purchase the blend to take home in a special keepsake tin.

Not that guests would want to return home. In addition to being treated like dignitaries by the staff of the Willard, guests are surrounded by nineteenth-century elegance, albeit with an updated touch.

During the restoration of the Willard in the 1980's, the intricate floor design was preserved through the installation of over a million mosaic tile pieces. The grand hall's marble doorframes were refinished and the beaux-arts moldings repaired. New marble thresholds replaced those that were missing, and the promenade's pilasters and marble stairs were returned to their original grandeur.

Although the site on which the Willard stands has served as a hostelry in some form since 1816, it wasn't until Henry and Edward Willard bought the property in 1850 that the hotel's legacy as a major social and political force in Washington began. While covering the Civil War for The Atlantic Monthly, Nathaniel Hawthorne wrote that the Willard "may be much more justly called the center of Washington and the Union than either the Capitol, the White House, or the State Department."

In 1861, upon hearing Union Soldiers singing "John Brown's Body" near her window, Julia Ward Howe wrote the words to "The Battle Hymn of the Republic." For nearly a month in 1923, President Coolidge used the Willard as his base of operations while waiting for the widowed Mrs. Harding to move from the White House. During this time, the presidential standard flew from the entrance.

Guests today at the Willard experience the finest in luxury accommodations. In addition to its fabulous Afternoon Tea service, the hotel offers 332 guest rooms, including 40 suites, 19,891 square feet of function space, the elegant Willard Room restaurant, Café 1401, the Round Robin Bar, and 24-hour private dining, laundry, business and fitness centers. From its inception to this day, the Willard has been a major force in the social and political life of Washington, D.C., and the Peacock Alley promenade continues to charm guests from around the world.

ℰ⟩Ɽ

The Willard InterContinental is located at 1401 Pennsylvania Avenue NW, Washington DC. Reservations are required for Afternoon Tea, served from 2:30 p.m. to 5:00 p.m. The last seating is at 4:30. For reservations, call 202-637-7350. www.washington.intercontinental.com

∾ RECITES ↝

They call it the "Residence of Presidents," and it's easy to see why. The Willard Inter-continental serves tea foods fit for a head of state.

The Chesapeake Bay is famous for its blue crab harvests. For a regional addition to the three-tiered tray, the Willard InterContinental serves up fresh blue crab on toasted brioche.

CHESAPEAKE BAY CRAB TEA SANDWICH ON TOASTED BRIOCHE
Makes 16 sandwiches

1	pound fresh jumbo lump crabmeat
2	tablespoons finely chopped fresh tarragon
2	tablespoons mayonnaise
1	tablespoon lemon juice
1	tablespoon lime juice
$1/4$	sea salt
$1/8$	teaspoon ground black pepper
1	loaf fresh brioche
Paprika	

1. Preheat oven to 400°.
2. In medium bowl, combine crabmeat and tarragon. Add mayonnaise, lemon juice, lime juice, salt, and pepper.
3. Slice brioche into $1/2$-inch slices. Using $2^1/2$-inch round cutter, cut 16 rounds of brioche and toast lightly in oven, about five minutes on each side.
4. Place 1 tablespoon of crab salad on top of bread and sprinkle with paprika.

CRANBERRY SCONES
Makes 18 scones

4	cups all purpose flour
$1^1/2$	tablespoons baking powder
$1/2$	teaspoon baking soda
$1/2$	cup granulated sugar
$3/4$	teaspoon salt
2	teaspoons ground cinnamon
1	cup cold unsalted butter, cubed
$3/4$	cup dried cranberries
1	large egg
$2/3$	cup buttermilk
1	teaspoon vanilla extract

1. Preheat oven to 400°. Line baking sheet with parchment paper.
2. In large mixing bowl, sift together flour, baking powder, baking soda, sugar, salt, and cinnamon. Using pastry blender, cut in butter until mixture is crumbly. Add cranberries.
3. In small bowl, combine egg, buttermilk and vanilla extract.
4. Form well in center of flour mixture. Add buttermilk mixture, stirring just until moistened.
5. On lightly floured surface, knead dough until combined. Do not overwork dough.
6. Roll dough out to ½-inch thickness. Cut into desired shapes.
7. Place on prepared baking sheet and brush with beaten egg. Bake 15-18 minutes, or until lightly browned.

CHOCOLATE DIPPED FLORENTINES

Makes 12 dozen cookies

6	tablespoons butter
⅓	cup plus 1 tablespoon honey
¼	cup Devonshire cream
1	cup plus 2 tablespoons granulated sugar
8	ounces candied mixed fruit, diced
¼	cup sliced almonds
½	cup slivered almonds
6	ounces semisweet chocolate

1. Line baking sheet with parchment paper.
2. In small saucepan over low heat, combine butter, honey, Devonshire cream, and sugar. Bring mixture to 230°; monitor with candy thermometer.
3. Add candied fruit, sliced almonds, and slivered almonds. Mix well.
4. Pour mixture onto prepared baking sheet. Allow to cool slightly.
5. Roll mixture into log shape. Wrap and freeze overnight.
6. Preheat oven to 350°. Line baking sheet with parchment paper.
7. Remove dough from freezer. Slice very thin. Place 2 inches apart on prepared baking sheet.
8. Bake 10-12 minutes, or until golden brown.
9. Melt chocolate in microwave on High at 30 second-intervals until chocolate melts. Cool. Dip half of each Florentine into melted chocolate. Place on paper-lined pan to set.

Note: If chocolate begins to harden, microwave at 10-second intervals until it reaches melting point.

Chocolate-dipped Florentines are an easy to make treat that will always impress your friends. These sweet treats will add visual charm to your tea menu.

WINDSOR COURT HOTEL
New Orleans, Louisiana

A warm scone and a steaming cup of tea can be enjoyed while the soothing sounds of a harp float in the air at the Windsor Court Hotel.

Aptly named, the Royal Tea served at Windsor Court Hotel in New Orleans is no mere serving of beverage and biscuits. It is, by design, a bit of a sanctuary for the soul.

Located on the lobby level of the Windsor, Le Salon has a single entrance, which adds to the ambience, offering at once a feeling of openness and intimacy. Decorated in restful but warm colors and floral accents, Le Salon is filled with ornate period reproduction pieces from the seventeenth and eighteenth centuries. Round-top tables that seat six or more sit comfortably side by side with tea tables ideal for smaller groups. Guests have their choice of loungeable upholstered wingback chairs or plump settees, as well as baccarat tables at teatime.

An impressibly trained staff begins preparing hours in advance each day for the English-style tea service. Servers at Le Salon are trained in etiquette, the history of tea, how to properly serve it, and how to stimulate conversation—a central element of the tea experience. Politics is a no-no, but more appropriate topics might include travel, family, and personal experiences. The staff at Le Salon also understands that part of good service is asking the right questions.

And as with any well-oiled (and well-heeled) production, timing is everything.

"The servers have their timing down perfectly. They understand the art and pleasure of tea, and never interrupt at the wrong moment," says harpist Rachel Van Voorhees. Serving as the principal harpist for the Louisiana Philharmonic

Orchestra, Rachel has also provided soothing chamber music to tea guests at the Windsor Court for nearly two decades.

"I don't know of many hotels in America that have made such a commitment to having fine music for guests. They've always made me feel at home here," Rachel says.

The Windsor has also made a commitment to providing guests with the very best tea and foods. The Classic Tea menu includes a choice of loose-leaf teas, blends, or tisanes, with a selection of sweets; a quartet of tea sandwiches; and two scones with Devonshire cream with lemon curd, jams and preserves prepared in-house from seasonal fruits and flavorings. For the Royal Tea, the service includes a starter of sherry, sparkling wine or chardonnay; and smoked salmon and sevruga caviar canapés; plus the foods and teas available with the Classic Tea.

In a single year, the Windsor Court kitchens produce more than 92,000 tea sandwiches alone. Classic examples and requested favorites include cucumber with dill and vinaigrette, roasted turkey with curried mayonnaise, poached Norwegian salmon with wasabi and caviar, and egg salad on artisan bread.

The menu of sweets allows for a bit more experimentation, as well as a chance for the Windsor's pastry chefs to flex their collective creative muscle. Must-haves, such as chocolate-dipped strawberries and truffles are offered, along with a varied selection of tartlets, petit fours, and pastries.

The Windsor Court Hotel, 300 Gravier Street, New Orleans, Louisiana. Tea is served in Le Salon Friday through Sunday, with two seating times, 2 and 4:30 p.m. Reservations are required. Call 504-596-4773. A special menu for children is also available upon request.

~RECIPES~

POACHED SALMON SALAD SANDWICHES • WINDSOR COURT HOTEL
WALNUT SCONES • EARL GREY TEA TRUFFLES

There's a reason they call it the Royal Tea; the food is fit for a queen. Save room for Earl Grey Tea Truffles, a delicious twist on an old favorite.

In a single year, the Windsor Court produces more than 92,000 tea sandwiches. These are our favorites.

POACHED SALMON SALAD SANDWICHES
Makes 3 cups salad

1³/₄ pounds salmon fillet, skin removed
2   tablespoons kosher salt
1   cup finely chopped red onion
¹/₂ cup finely chopped chives
¹/₄ cup fresh lemon juice
¹/₄ cup finely chopped chervil or parsley
¹/₄ cup extra virgin olive oil
2   tablespoons Dijon mustard
2   tablespoons chopped capers
1   tablespoon yellow curry powder
¹/₄ teaspoon salt
¹/₈ teaspoon ground white pepper
Rye bread
Garnish: capers, chives

1. Cut salmon into 2x2-inch pieces.
2. In large saucepan, bring 3 quarts water to boil. Add salmon and salt; poach 2 minutes. Drain and chill.
3. In work bowl of food processor, place salmon; pulse 2 minutes.
4. Add onion, chives, lemon juice, chervil or parsley, olive oil, mustard, capers, curry powder, salt, and pepper. Pulse about 30 seconds, or until mixture is mousse-like in texture. Refrigerate.
5. Preheat oven to 300°.
6. Using 1³/₄-inch round cutter, cut as many rye rounds as desired (1 slice bread will yield about 3 rounds). Toast bread on both sides; cool completely.
7. Using pastry bag fitted with medium star tip, pipe salmon onto toasted rye rounds. Garnish with capers and chives, if desired.

WINDSOR COURT HOTEL WALNUT SCONES
Makes 8 scones

2   cups plus 2 tablespoons all-purpose flour
¼   cup sugar
1½   teaspoons baking powder
½   teaspoon salt
¼   cup walnuts, chopped
6   tablespoons butter
¾   cup buttermilk

1. In medium bowl, combine flour, sugar, baking powder, salt, and walnuts. Using pastry blender, cut in butter until mixture is crumbly.
2. Add buttermilk, stirring just until combined. Gently fold in extra flour if needed, until dough can be rolled.
3. On lightly floured surface, roll dough to 1-inch thickness; chill 30 minutes.
4. Preheat oven to 350°. Line baking sheet with parchment paper.
5. Using knife, cut dough into 8 wedges or desired shapes.
6. Bake 15-20 minutes, or until scones are golden brown and wooden pick inserted near center comes out clean.

EARL GREY TEA TRUFFLES
Makes about 60 truffles

½   cup heavy cream
½   cup milk
2½   tablespoons Earl Grey tea (or about 7 tea bags)
12   ounces dark chocolate, chopped
8   ounces milk chocolate, chopped
1½   cups cocoa powder

1. In medium saucepan, combine cream, milk, and tea. Bring to boil. Remove from heat and steep 10 minutes.
2. In medium bowl, strain mixture through fine sieve or cheesecloth.
3. In seperate bowl, combine dark and milk chocolates.
4. Return mixture to saucepan; bring mixture to boil and pour over dark and milk chocolates, stirring mixture gently until chocolate is completely melted.
5. Place in airtight container in freezer. Chill thoroughly.
6. Using small ice cream scoop, dip small amount chocolate ganache mixture. Using hands, roll ganache to form 1-inch balls. Coat truffles with cocoa powder.

Note: Chill until ready for use.

Earl Grey Tea combined with dark and milk chocolates ... need anything else be said? These truffles are melt-in-your-mouth delicious.

WOODLANDS RESORT & INN
Summerville, South Carolina

Woodlands Resort & Inn is a step ahead in luxury while also being a step back in time. Modern amenities paired with Old-World charm make this a place you won't want to leave.

Just as you convince yourself that you have somehow missed a turn on Parsons Road in Summerville, South Carolina, and that you are lost in the beautiful but still unfamiliar backwoods of the Lowcountry, there it is. "Woodland Resort and Inn" the sign reads. At last.

If it's a grand hideaway you seek for your afternoon tea experience or a leisurely weekend stay, you're in luck at Woodlands. The five-star resort has mastered the art of exclusivity, from its physical locale, to its tony furnishings, to its shrewdly trained staff. Boasting a battery of amenities, services and leisure activities, Woodlands offers a unique fusion of Southern hospitality, European flair, and breezy, island-inspired charm that serves to create a soothing ambience for Afternoon Tea.

"Our setting offers a sense of serenity, charm, and natural beauty to provide the ultimate in relaxation for our guests wanting to escape the pressure of daily life," says Woodlands spokesman Doug Lester. "We have assembled a staff of international hoteliers and blended them with our genteel Southerners to create an environment where guests are treated as if they're being welcomed into our homes and will feel, in a short time, that they are a part of our Woodlands family."

That same sense of serenity and charm also infuses the English-style tea service at Woodlands. Available Monday through Saturday from 3:30 to 5 p.m. to in-house guests upon request and to visitors by reservation, the tea boasts a "spontaneous menu" courtesy of the inn's executive chef

Tarver King. A confirmed fan of both Earl Grey and gunpowder greens, Tarver says the tea menu tends to change daily, based on the whim of the chef and, more importantly, the season.

"We have farmers bringing in produce fresh off the vine daily through the kitchen door, so we try to keep in tune with the flow of what's in season," the chef says.

The tea menu always includes four savories—typically one hot sandwich, one vegetarian offering and two purely chef-inspired creations. Spanakopita has appeared on Woodland's three-tiered trays, along with truffled grilled cheese and fennelled salami sandwiches, sundry quiches and tartlets, and a perennial favorite, the inn's signature pimiento cheese. The secret ingredient? Homemade mascarpone cheese, Tarver reveals.

Scones, curds, clotted cream, preserves and a palette of handcrafted sweets round out the Afternoon Tea menu, and, upon request, the staff will gladly recommend a tea selection. In fact, Tarver maintains that an expert pairing of beverage and food is essential to the tea experience.

"Some flavors can be too strong and overpower the tea. You don't want the food to take away from the tea or the tea to take away from the food," the chef says. "We have found that sweets tend to bring out the fragrance of the tea, while salty foods tend to heighten the flavor of the tea. We try to play with those ideas in our tea menu, to give guests the best possible pairing."

ᘒᘒᘒ

Woodlands Resort & Inn is located at 125 Parsons Road, Summerville, South Carolina. Afternoon Tea is served Monday through Saturday, 3 p.m. to 5 p.m. Reservations made 24 hours in advance are required. Call 843-308-2115. www.woodlandsinn.com

~❧ RECIPES ❧~

Chef Tarver King works diligently to ensure that the food he creates at Woodlands Resort and Inn does not overpower tea and vice versa. The following recipes are designed to complement the tea for a truly palatable experience.

Truffle oil is the 'secret' ingredient in this new interpretation of the grilled cheese sandwich. Tomato marmalade and fontina cheese add sophisticated taste.

TRUFFLE GRILLED CHEESE FINGER SANDWICHES WITH TOMATO MARMALADE
Makes 12 sandwiches

12 slices fontina cheese
12 thin slices Italian soppresatta, or salami of choice
8 slices sourdough bread, crusts removed
Tomato Marmalade (recipe follows)
Truffle oil
Salt and ground black pepper to taste
Butter

1. Place 3 slices each of fontina cheese and salami on four bread slices.
2. Spread tomato marmalade over top; drizzle with truffle oil. Season to taste with salt and pepper. Top with four remaining slices of bread.
3. In medium non-stick skillet over low heat, melt butter. Grill sandwiches at low heat until golden brown and crisp.
4. Slice each sandwich into fingers.

TOMATO MARMALADE
Makes 2 cups

1 (28-ounce) can whole tomatoes, drained, seeded, and chopped
2 cups minced red onion
¾ cup minced shallot

1½ cups sugar
1 cup red wine vinegar
⅛ teaspoon salt

In large saucepan, combine tomatoes, onion, shallot, sugar, vinegar, and salt. Bring to boil; reduce heat to medium-low. Simmer 1 hour, or until thick, stirring occasionally. Refrigerate until cool.

CINNAMON SHORTBREAD
Makes about 24 cookies

½ cup unsalted butter
¼ cup sugar
Pinch salt
1 teaspoon cinnamon
1 teaspoon vanilla extract
1½ cups all-purpose flour
Cinnamon sugar

Shortbread cookie left-overs can be crumbled and frozen for later use in a pie or cheesecake crust.

1. In medium bowl and using electric mixer at low speed, beat together butter and sugar until light and creamy. Add salt, cinnamon, and vanilla extract. Gradually add flour; stirring just until combined.
2. On lightly floured surface, knead dough lightly once or twice to incorporate all ingredients (do not overwork dough).
3. Dough may be chilled 1-2 hours.
4. Preheat oven to 350°. Line 15x10x1-inch jellyroll pan with parchment paper.
5. Press dough into prepared pan. Prick with fork to prevent puffing.
6. Sprinkle with cinnamon sugar; bake 8 minutes.
7. Remove from oven and cut into squares while still in pan. Cool 10 minutes; remove from pan.

Note: Oven times may vary due to size and shape of shortbread. Thinner cookies should require no more than 6-8 minutes total baking time.

Sprinkling the shortbread with cinnamon sugar prior to baking adds crunchy texture and visual appeal to the cookies.

DRIED FRUIT SCONES
Makes 16 scones

1½ cups all-purpose flour
½   teaspoon salt
2½ teaspoons baking powder
2   tablespoons plus 1 teaspoon sugar, divided
6   tablespoons unsalted butter
½   cup mixed dried fruit
1   large egg
½   cup heavy cream
1   teaspoon vanilla extract

1. In large bowl, combine flour, salt, baking powder, and 2 tablespoons sugar. Using pastry blender, cut in butter until crumbly. Mix in dried fruit.
2. In small bowl, combine egg, cream, and vanilla extract. Add to flour mixture, mixing just until moistened.
3. Wrap dough in plastic wrap; refrigerate 1-3 hours.
4. Preheat oven to 350°. Line baking sheet with parchment paper.
5. On lightly floured surface, roll dough to 2-inch thickness. Using 2-inch round cutter, cut scones; place on prepared baking sheet.
6. Sprinkle tops with 1 teaspoon sugar and bake 12-15 minutes, or until golden brown.

LEMON CURD
Makes about 2½ cups

¾   cup lemon juice
1½ cups sugar
10 tablespoons butter
4   large eggs

1. In medium saucepan, combine lemon juice, sugar, and butter. Bring to boil.
2. In medium bowl, whisk eggs. Temper by slowly adding hot lemon juice mixture to eggs.
3. Pour mixture back into saucepan and whisk over low heat 1-2 minutes until mixture thickens.
4. Strain mixture and refrigerate. Keep refrigerated up to 10 days.

Using mixed dried fruit in these scones gives them an exotic flavor that will complement most tea blends. If you prefer, experiment with your favorite dried fruit to find one you like best.

RECIPE INDEX

~ADDRESS BOOK~

BOOK JACKET FRONT COVER
• Teapot, cup and saucer~Columbia Sage Green by Wedgwood. Dessert plate~Yuletide by Waterford. All available at Bromberg's, 2800 Cahaba Road, Mountain Brook, AL 35223 (205) 871-3276
• Flowers by Dorothy McDaniel's Flower Market, 2560 18th Street South, Birmingham, AL 35209, (205) 871-0092

APPLE CAKE TEA ROOM
• Le Jacquard linens~available at Christine's, 2822 Petticoat Lane, Mountain Brook, AL 35223, (205) 871-8297
• Teapot~available at Stein Mart, *www.steinmart.com* 664 Montgomery Highway, Vestavia Hills, AL 35216, (205) 823-0686
• China~privately owned

THE CAROLINA INN
• China~available at HomeGoods, 800-614-HOME, *www.homegoods.com*

1891 CEDAR CREST VICTORIAN INN
• China~available at HomeGoods, 800-614-HOME, *www.homegoods.com*

CHARLESTON PLACE
• China~privately owned (Bombay dinnerware by John Maddock & Sons, Made in England)

THE ENGLISH ROSE TEA ROOM
• Teapot and Magenta china~available at HomeGoods, 800-614-HOME, *www.homegoods.com*
• Chelsea Luster dinnerware by MacKenzie Childs~ available at Christine's, 2822 Petticoat Lane, Mountain Brook, AL 35223, (205) 871-8297
• Blue glassware~available at Anthropologie, The Summit, 200 Summit Boulevard, Birmingham, AL 35243-3107, (205) 298-9929, *www.anthropologie.com*

THE FAIRMONT OLYMPIC HOTEL
• China and linens~available at HomeGoods, 800-614-HOME, *www.homegoods.com*

FOUR SEASONS HOTEL PHILADELPHIA
• China~privately owned

GRACIE'S ENGLISH TEAROOM
• Ivory Scroll platter~available at Stein Mart, 664 Montgomery Highway, Vestavia Hills, AL 35216, (205) 823-0686, *www.steinmart.com*
• Ivory cake stand~available at HomeGoods, 800-614-HOME, *www.homegoods.com*
• Red transferware~privately owned

THE HERMITAGE HOTEL
• China~privately owned (Henley by Minton)

KATHLEEN'S TEA ROOM & DAY SPA
• China~privately owned

THE LADIES OF LUCERNE TEA ROOM
• Dinnerware Available at World Market, 877-WORLDMARKET, *www.worldmarket.com*
• Linens~privately owned
• Nantucket Basket by Wedgwood teacup and saucer~available at *www.wedgwoodusa.com*, 800-955-1550

MARTIN HOUSE INN
• China and basket~privately owned

MISS MABLE'S TEAROOM
• China and linens~available at World Market, 877-WORLDMARKET, *www.worldmarket.com*

MISS ROSEMARIE'S SPECIAL TEAS
• China and linens~available at Stein Mart, 664 Montgomery Highway, Vestavia Hills, AL 35216 (205) 823-0686, *www.steinmart.com*
• Flowers by Tana Avery of Dorothy McDaniel's Flower Market, 2560 18th Street South, Birmingham, AL 35209, (205) 871-0092

THE RITTENHOUSE HOTEL
• Brown Transferware china~available at HomeGoods, 800-614-HOME, *www.homegoods.com*
• Cappuccino dessert plates and beaded linens~available at Stein Mart, 664 Montgomery Highway, Vestavia Hills, AL 35216, (205) 823-0686, *www.steinmart.com*

WILLARD INTERCONTINENTAL WASHINGTON
• Ivory Wicker cake pedestal~available at Christine's, 2822 Petticoat Lane, Mountain Brook, AL 35223, (205) 871-8297
• Ivory Lace dinnerware~available at HomeGoods, 800-614-HOME, *www.homegoods.com*

WINDSOR COURT HOTEL
• China~privately owned

WOODLANDS RESORT & INN
•China~available at Anthropologie, The Summit, 200 Summit Boulevard, Birmingham, AL 35243-3107, (205) 298-9929, *www.anthropologie.com*